BRENDA GANTT

Linger Around the Table Y'all

RECIPES & STORIES TO SHARE WITH FAMILY & FRIENDS

83
PRESS

83 Press
2323 2nd Avenue North
Birmingham, AL 35203
83press.com

ISBN: 978-0-9794090-7-3
Printed in the USA.

BRENDA GANTT

Linger Around the Table Y'all

RECIPES & STORIES TO SHARE WITH FAMILY & FRIENDS

INTRODUCTION

Dear family and friends,

I can't believe that my second cookbook has been finished and is ready for use! It has truly been a labor of love. Wanting to save these old Southern recipes for the generations that will come after us has been my goal. I needed to leave something positive behind.

Within the pages of this book, you'll find some special details I am thrilled to share with you. Taking time to create and enjoy your gifts from God is a wonderful way to find joy, and that is why the illustrations you'll see at the beginning of each chapter are my very own artwork. You'll also notice the "Apron Strings" boxes. The aprons shown are all a part of my collection, and many of them my special friends—you—have sent to me.

I encourage you to write all your family recipes in your own hand. Your children and grandchildren will be so glad you took the time and effort. Remember to also sign your name under each recipe you write and include any stories you have that go with the recipes.

It's important to linger around the table, cook together as a family, and to make the kitchen a place that holds special memories for your family. I hope the recipes included here will help you do just that.

This book has been a blessing from the Lord to me, my children, and grandchildren. I pray it will be a blessing to my faithful followers, too. Cooking in my little red kitchen with you all is a true joy.

FOR GOD HATH NOT GIVEN US THE SPIRIT OF FEAR,
BUT OF POWER, AND OF LOVE, AND OF A SOUND MIND.
—2 TIMOTHY 1:7, KJV

So, linger around the table, y'all, and ask God to bless the ones who are gathered around it.

Linger!

Brenda Gantt

CONTENTS

DEDICATION

God's command for us is to leave our father and mother and cleave to our mate. George and I did just that. We cleaved to each other for 50 wonderful years. No, it wasn't always easy. There were many trials and disagreements along the way.

There were some nights when we went to bed with anger in our hearts—not even able to say, "I'm sorry." We'd each pull the cover up high around our necks and be very careful not to let even our toes touch each other. What a silly thing for grown adults to do. It didn't take long before we realized our faults. Life is too short to stay angry, so we'd say, "I'm sorry" with a tight hug and kiss, and we'd make up. We'd wake up the next morning refreshed and renewed.

Life with my soulmate was fulfilling in every aspect. He was my best friend, my encourager, and my life's love. After three years of blissful moments, we followed God's command again. We prayed, "Dear Father, may the next generation be blessed as I have been blessed. Amen."

Genesis 9:1 says, "And God blessed Noah and his sons, and said to them, 'Be fruitful and multiply and fill the earth.'" George and I both liked that command—so, we got busy multiplying! We were blessed with our baby boy, Dallas. He was healthy, beautiful, blue-eyed, and was always diaper-wetting and hungry. Not knowing much about being a mama, he made me realize that I better learn—and learn QUICK!

As a little one, Dallas held his breath until he passed out when he got mad. He hid in the showcase windows of the Penney's department store, followed the beagle dogs off into the woods, and would ride on my hip as I hung out clothes on the line. As he became a teenager, he was known for his love of sporty cars, spending time in the woods, and being extra hungry. My greatest blessings have come since he has become a man, caring father, faithful husband, church leader, people-encourager, and counselor to me. He's genuine, hardworking, and a leader. I'm mighty proud to be his mama.

Two years later we were blessed again! This time, with a prissy, brown-eyed, gentle, precious baby girl who we named Hannah. We were overwhelmed with her beauty and gentle disposition. She was easygoing and hardly ever made a fuss or cried. But there was one thing she didn't like . . . to be rocked. I was bound and determined to make her like rocking. I won, and to this day, that daughter of mine loves rocking and swinging as she glances at nature from her back porch. That gentle spirit erupted as a teenager. We watched her like a hawk trying to keep her out of mischief. But, oh glory, what a fine woman she became. She's trustworthy and tells it like it is. Hannah is a wonderful mama, wife, and friend. She's someone I can count on through thick and thin. We have all learned not to ask her opinion about anything unless we really want to hear the truth. She's a Proverbs 31 woman for sure! I love being her mama!

I proudly dedicate my second cookbook, *Linger Around the Table Y'all*, to my faithful husband George Patton Gantt, my wise son Dallas Patton Gantt, and my devoted daughter Hannah Maria Gantt Merrell.

HOME HAS A HEART IN IT

FOREWORD BY DALLAS GANTT

A special place of love, faith, and family growth—the heart of our home was the kitchen. I remember the sights, sounds, and smells of our kitchen when I was growing up. My mama had a huge rocking chair over by the kitchen table that I would sit in while I watched her work her magic. As she worked, I rocked. We would talk about all aspects of life, sometimes singing along with the church hymns playing on the radio. All our family and friends would seek out that kitchen for great food and fellowship.

The kitchen is where we met for Sunday dinner and carried on wonderful conversations. Those conversations always ended up on a funny topic that I shouldn't put in this book, but our family will remember them. A lot of my boyhood memories involved sitting around the table and molded me into the man I am today. The godly wisdom my sister and I received from my mama and daddy was priceless.

Both my mother and daddy worked very hard to make the kitchen the heart of our home. The kitchen table was where we forged our family bond and created great relationships with each other. We talked about life over country cooking—leaving nothing left unsaid no matter how sensitive the topic. As a teenager, my friends and I sat around the kitchen table playing cards while Mama fixed us something to eat along with the best sweet tea you've ever had. We never sat in the other rooms of the house. We just hung around the kitchen because that's where all the food was. The smiles and laughter of that special place was like nowhere else on earth.

When I visit Mama now, the first thing she asks when I walk through the door is, "Do you want something to eat? I have supper on the stove." We don't sit in the living room to talk, but rather, we sit in the kitchen. When friends come to see Mama, they sit at the kitchen table to talk, too. It is just the natural place in her home for loved ones to gather. To this day, it is the heart of the home, and it beats as strong as ever.

The kitchen's heart beats because of Mama and how she formed it into a place of refuge and refueling for the soul. As you read through this cookbook, my hope is that it encourages you to form your kitchen into the heart of your home and to forge your own lifelong memories there, too.

BIG MAMA'S TABLE

The supper table is for:

1. Holding hands while saying the blessing
2. Winding down after a long, busy day
3. Sharing dreams and desires
4. Having easy conversations with one another
5. Planning trips, vacations, or adventures
6. Lifting and encouraging each other
7. Laughing, talking, and enjoying being together
8. Teaching table manners through example
9. Bonding with all who sit with you
10. Lingering with a cup of coffee or another glass of tea

The supper table is not for:

1. Using technology, phones, or TVs
2. Discussing finances, bad grades, or how poorly one has performed in sports, work, school, or life
3. Baseball caps or shirtless men
4. One person to dominate the conversation
5. Swallowing your food whole so you can leave the table
6. Bringing your bad attitude and poochy mouth
7. Criticizing the meal
8. Leaving the table before telling the cook you enjoyed it

I'LL FLY AWAY

I'm sitting in the front seat of my Ford pickup truck. The windows are rolled down to let the gentle breeze blow across the seat. My eyes are wanting to shut as I didn't sleep well last night. But, through the crack in my eyes, I watch the brown sagebrush bend and dance in the sun. Some old buzzards are soaring high in the clear blue sky looking for lunch. The new-planted pines are dancing, too, with their green bushy tops. Longleaf pines not more than 10 feet high will one day be made into lumber to build someone a first home, or a light pole, or maybe a fence for horses.

Life seems to just fly by. Long after I'm gone, the sagebrush and pines will still be on the landscape. The buzzards will still be soaring, and eyes will still be sleepy. As I rest here in the truck, I wonder if I'm making a difference in the lives of others. Have I influenced my grandchildren for the good or the bad? I hope they would look at my mistakes and shortcomings and be better people than I. But, in reality, we will all go through some really hard times because we can't seem to learn from the mistakes of others.

Even if I live a long life, eternity is not far away. My life has been filled with experiences and moments—some great ones and some I'd just as soon forget. But mostly, my years have been just regular moments of life, love, work, and play. Out of all the memories I possess, one stands out among all the rest: my Savior, my Lord, my God. He alone has seen me through some very hard times. He alone has protected me, guided me, and loved me even when I was not lovely at all. I'm thankful He sent the Holy Spirit to convict me of my sinful heart. I'm thankful I surrendered my life to Him. One day, I'll fly away just like the old song says. I'll leave behind the ones I hold so dear to my heart. But, I know I will see them again at the throne of God. Life has been good. I have been truly blessed!

chapter 1

THE SUPPER TABLE

IF THE TABLE COULD TALK

How thankful our family has always been for our supper table. It's not a granite bar with shiny stools or a long island with everyone sitting on one side. Our table is a plain old wooden table that belonged to George's great-grandparents. We sit round about it, first praying over our supper and then talking, eating, laughing, and enjoying our time together. One good thing about eating at the table is that we are looking directly into the eyes of the ones we love. Through the years, you learn to read the eyes. You know whether those eyes are troubled, happy, excited, or anxious.

When George and I first married, he sat at the head, and I sat right by his side. I remember the day we got the table. We turned on the water hose, got a broom and soap, and gave it a good bath before we brought it into the house. It was dirty and had stains, dinks, old square nails, and even a smooth spot. I guess someone had rubbed their hand over that spot for years—it was as smooth as a baby's little butt. Now, it was our time to make memories around this old table. It wasn't long before we were pulling up an old wooden high chair for our first baby, Dallas. In two years, Hannah was the next to grace our table. We sat around it eating and talking to those two babies even before they could talk back.

The table has a ½-inch crack right down the middle with two pegs holding the two wide boards together. If we had peas, rice, or crumbly cookies, you can imagine what happened—all that food wound up falling through the crack and onto the floor. There were many nights after I got the babies asleep in their beds that I found myself crawling under that old supper table wiping up all the crumblies that fell through the crack. As old as that table is, I bet I wasn't the first mama who wound up doing the very same thing when her children made messes.

Praying Grandbabies
2022
B. Gantt

Years later, our family grew. Dallas married Anna, and Hannah married Walt. Now, we have a table full of loves—the grandbabies—Bay, Isabella, Cape, William, and Banks. There is endless talking, bonding, storytelling, and love at the supper table. We all miss Big Daddy (George), as he is at the Lord's table now. But we still talk and tell stories about Big Daddy and his crazy adventures. I think that telling stories about those who have gone before us is important to the little ones. It helps them know about their connection to the family. But, through it all, one thing remains the same—eating supper at our old wooden table and looking into the eyes of those we love has made our bond even tighter. The supper table did its job! It brought our growing family together.

POT ROAST

———————

I just love Pot Roast, especially for Sunday lunch. It's a great meal for feeding lots of children. When you brown the meat on all sides, it seals in the juices. You want to keep the gravy kind of thin. Continue to add a little water, a little at a time, if needed.

Salt and black pepper to taste
1   (3- to 4-pound) beef roast (chuck or round)
1½ cups White Lily all-purpose flour, divided
¾   cup vegetable oil
2   cups water (or more if needed to thin)
1   (1-ounce) package dry onion soup mix
Cooked russet potatoes
Cooked carrots

1. Preheat oven to 350°.
2. Sprinkle salt and pepper on both sides of the roast. In a large bowl, dredge roast in 1 cup flour, coating all sides.
3. In a deep cast-iron skillet, heat oil over medium-low heat. Gently add roast to oil in skillet and cook until medium brown on bottom. Using a spatula or kitchen tongs, turn roast and brown all remaining sides. Remove roast from skillet and set aside.
4. In the remaining oil in skillet, add remaining ½ cup flour and cook over medium heat. Stir constantly with a spatula to mix flour and oil together. When flour mixture becomes a medium brown color, add 2 cups water, stirring to combine, and cook another 1 to 2 minutes. Add onion soup mix, stirring well. If gravy is too thick, add more water, a little at a time. Put the roast in the gravy.
5. Cover with a lid, and pop in the oven. Bake for 2 hours. Serve with potatoes and carrots.

EVERY KIND OF BEASTS, AND OF BIRDS, AND OF SERPENTS, AND OF THINGS

IN THE SEA IS TAMED, AND HATH BEEN TAMED BY MANKIND.

BUT THE TONGUE CAN NO MAN TAME; IT IS AN UNRULY EVIL,

FULL OF DEADLY POISON.

—JAMES 3: 7–8, KJV

CLOTH NAPKINS

When my grandchildren set the table for me, they all know to get out the cloth napkins. I've got several colors— white, red, light and dark green, checked—and special napkins made out of an old tablecloth. My Big Mama made them when I was just a little girl. To me, they are beautiful. So, I only use them on special occasions. They are covered with pink and purple flowers with pretty green leaves. My Big Mama crocheted delicate lace around the edge of each napkin. When you wipe your mouth, you can feel the softness of the gentle, old cotton. It's like putting on your favorite old T-shirt. The one that lets you know you're at home and can now relax—pure joy!

I was raised with cloth napkins, real plates, and real tea glasses. Mama didn't use any paper products much, only paper towels when frying fish and chicken. I do the same at my home—only cloth napkins here. I, like my mama, rarely use paper towels— we even dry our hands with dish towels. I love the feeling of cotton cloth napkins. They are absorbent, soft, and reusable! I think everybody needs at least two sets!

LUNCH BUNCH

I'm in a group called the Lunch Bunch. We meet at a different restaurant every week for a great meal and lots of laugher and conversation. One particular time, I had used up that cheap, flimsy, thin napkin that was provided at the restaurant. One of our ladies, Pat, who is never short on words, asked the waitress to bring extra napkins. By the time she got back to our table, I had knocked over my glass of tea. We were all scrambling to get out of the way of flying tea! The table was soaked and so were we! The waitress then had to bring a dishcloth to get up all the liquid. If we had been provided with a cloth napkin, I doubt this catastrophe would have ever happened!

Brenda's Lunch Bunch

DIRTY RICE

*Quick, easy, and delicious, Dirty Rice goes with any meat you might fix,
and it's good for covered dish suppers, too.*

1   (10.5-ounce) can French onion soup
1   (10.5-ounce) can beef consommé
1   cup white rice
1   (6-ounce) jar sliced mushrooms (drained)
½   stick salted butter (melted)

1. Preheat oven to 400°.
2. Combine all ingredients together in a 2-quart casserole dish.
3. Cover and bake for 45 minutes. Reduce oven temperature to 350°. Uncover and bake for 15 minutes more.

KITCHEN WISDOM

To make this a one-pot meal, you can put boneless pork chops on top of your rice. It will all cook together and be a wonderful way to feed your family!

CHICKEN POT PIE

Talk about a one-pot soul food meal—this is truly it. After you try it for the first time, your mouth will start watering just thinking about it! You can chop the vegetables and make the dough a day in advance and then put it together when you're ready to pop it in the oven.

1 (5-pound) whole chicken (cleaned)
6 large carrots (cut into circles)
Dumpling Dough
Salt and black pepper to taste
1 (15-ounce) can sweet English peas (drained)
5 hard-cooked eggs (sliced)
3 tablespoons salted butter (softened)

1. In a large pot, cover chicken with salted water and bring to a boil over medium-high heat; cook until tender. Remove the chicken. Drain and save the broth (about 8 cups). Shred chicken, discarding the skin and bones, and set aside.
2. In a medium pot, cover carrots with water and bring to a boil over medium-high heat; cook until almost tender. (Make sure not to boil too long or they will tear up.) Set aside.
3. Divide Dumpling Dough into 3 portions. Roll out 1 dough portion as thin as possible. Cut into strips.
4. In the same large pot, bring broth, salt, and pepper to a rolling boil over medium-high heat. Immediately start dropping the dumplings into the broth mixture.
5. Quickly roll out another dough portion. Cut into strips and drop dumplings into the broth mixture with the other dumplings. Cook 10 to 15 minutes. Remove dumplings from broth with a slotted utensil and reserve broth.

6. Preheat oven to 350°.
7. In a deep 14x11-inch (4-quart) casserole dish, layer the items in the following order: dumplings, carrots, peas, eggs, and chicken. Repeat 3 times until mixture reaches the top of the dish. Pour about 4 to 5 cups dumpling broth to 1 inch from top.
8. Roll out remaining dough portion to form crust. Place on top of the casserole and smear 3 tablespoons butter on top.
9. Bake until golden brown, about 30 minutes.

DUMPLING DOUGH

3 cups White Lily all-purpose flour
1 cup whole buttermilk
½ cup solid grease

1. Mix flour, buttermilk, and grease in a bowl. Knead together well. Keep adding a little bit of flour at a time until the dough is no longer sticky.
2. On a floured surface, take the dough out of the bowl. Knead on the surface until you have a firm ball of dough. This is when you will decide if you need to sprinkle more flour on the dough.
3. Roll out the dough as thin as possible. Try lifting the dough from the surface. If it sticks to the surface, that means to roll it back into a ball and add a little more flour at a time until just right.

KITCHEN WISDOM

Inside the cavity of the chicken, you're going to find all sorts of goodies, like a heart, gizzard, liver, and neck. George's mother always fried the neck with the skin on.
The gizzard is solid muscle, so it's really good for you.

CHICKEN POT PIE
You can do this, y'all!

When the dumplings have finished cooking, you'll layer your ingredients in your casserole dish, starting with the dumplings. You'll add in the vegetables, eggs, and chicken (repeat three times). Then, you'll pour some of the dumpling broth into the casserole dish—don't skimp on this part. The warm broth is what makes the dish so comforting! Lastly, roll out that final portion of dough and place it on top of the Chicken Pot Pie filling. Don't worry about getting the edges just right. You're making a home-cooked meal for your family, and it should look homemade! It's always better than store-bought, anyway!

Save the third portion of your dough for topping the Chicken Pot Pie. (The topping is probably everyone's favorite part!)

JAMBALAYA

Looking for something different? Everything but the kitchen sink goes in this fabulous pot of Jambalaya. I've even made it with leftover turkey and turkey broth from Thanksgiving—the sky's the limit!

½ pound smoked link sausage
½ cup diced bacon
2 pounds shrimp (fresh or thawed frozen)
1 tablespoon White Lily all-purpose flour
1 medium onion (chopped)
1 small green bell pepper (chopped)
2 small garlic cloves (finely chopped)
1 tablespoon Worcestershire sauce
½ teaspoon salt
½ teaspoon ground red pepper
1 tablespoon paprika
2 (16-ounce) cans diced tomatoes (undrained)
Hot cooked white rice

1. Cut sausage into circles. Soft fry in a skillet and let drain on paper towels. In the same skillet, cook bacon and let drain on paper towels.
2. Peel and clean shrimp.
3. In a large pot, add cooked sausage and bacon. Sprinkle flour over sausage and bacon. Stir. Add onion, bell pepper, garlic, Worcestershire, salt, red pepper, paprika, and tomatoes; cook over medium heat until mixture is kind of thick, stirring constantly.
4. When mixture is ready, stir in shrimp and cook until pink. Serve hot over white rice.

Grandbabies having fun

Grandbabies saying the blessing

DIETER'S EGGPLANT PARMESAN

This is a great diet food. Just look at the ingredients! It's delicious but not loaded with fat. You don't have to tell your family it's healthy, though—they'll never know!

1 large eggplant
4 egg whites
4 tablespoons water
1 (8-ounce) container grated Parmesan cheese
Garlic powder to taste
1 (8-ounce) jar low-carb marinara sauce

1. Preheat oven to 400°. Spray a large baking sheet with cooking spray.
2. Peel and cut eggplant into ¼-inch-thick slices.
3. In a shallow dish, beat egg whites and 4 tablespoons water until frothy. Pour the Parmesan into a shallow pie plate.

Dredge both sides of the eggplant slices in the egg white mixture and then press both sides of the eggplant in the Parmesan, coating each side.
4. Place coated eggplant slices onto prepared baking sheet. Sprinkle with garlic powder to taste and spray eggplant with cooking spray.
5. Bake for 20 minutes. Remove from oven. Using a spatula, turn eggplant and bake until brown, 10 minutes more.
6. Remove eggplant from the baking sheet and place in an 8x8-inch casserole dish. Cover with marinara sauce and sprinkle with Parmesan from dredge. Bake until hot, 10 minutes more.

HEALTHY LIVING

When George had to lose weight because of heart issues, this dish was one that we found that really helped. We were trying to eat healthy but didn't want to sacrifice taste and flavor. This dish was the perfect choice.

KITCHEN WISDOM

This meal can feel fancy! Next time you need a dish for a date night at home, make this recipe and serve it on a candlelit table. You'll feel like you're at a nice restaurant—without the restaurant price!

ANNA'S CHICKEN & RICE

On a cold winter night, this pot of chicken and rice will warm the whole body. It's a favorite of Cape's.

1 (4-pound) whole chicken (cleaned and skin removed as much as possible)
8 to 10 cups water
1 large onion (chopped)
1 (22.6-ounce) can cream of chicken soup
Salt and black pepper to taste
1 (8-ounce) container sour cream
Hot cooked rice

1. Place chicken in a pot large enough for whole chicken to sit in bottom with a tad bit of room around it. Cover chicken with about 8 to 10 cups water and bring to a boil over medium-high heat. Add chopped onion. Cover with a lid and reduce heat to low and simmer. Cook until chicken is very tender, 45 minutes to 1 hour. Remove chicken and set aside to let cool. (The broth needs to measure 8 cups. Add more water, if needed.)

2. Add soup to chicken broth in pot and stir until combined. Add salt and pepper to taste. Cook over low heat.

3. Place sour cream in a small bowl. Add ¼ cup broth mixture to sour cream and stir until smooth. Repeat 2 to 3 times, stirring to prevent sour cream from curdling. Add sour cream mixture back to broth mixture in pot and stir to combine.

4. Shred chicken, discarding bones, and add to pot. Add more water if the mixture is too thick for your taste.

5. Serve over hot cooked rice. This dish also goes great with steamed broccoli, green beans, or sweet peas.

WHATSOEVER THINGS ARE
TRUE
HONEST
JUST
PURE
LOVELY
GOOD REPORT
IF THERE BE ANY VIRTUE, AND IF THERE BE ANY PRAISE,
THINK ON THESE THINGS.

—PHILIPPIANS 4:8, KJV

Dallas and Anna

ONION CASSEROLE

You know how much I love onions, so this dish is right up my alley! A sweet, older lady, Mrs. Jane McGukin, who is a member of our church, Bethany Baptist, used to make an onion casserole for our Homecoming celebration, and I always loved it. I decided to try to make a casserole like it myself!

5   large Vidalia onions (sliced)
1   stick salted butter (melted)
1   (4-ounce) package cream cheese (softened)
⅓   cup whole milk
4   strips bacon (cooked and crumbled)
1   (4-ounce) jar diced pimentos (drained)
1   teaspoon salt
1   teaspoon black pepper
1   cup grated sharp Cheddar cheese

1. Preheat oven to 400°.
2. Place onions in a 3-quart casserole dish and drizzle with melted butter.
3. In a large bowl, mix together cream cheese, milk, bacon, pimentos, salt, and pepper. (The mixture should be thick like a paste.) Spread cream cheese mixture over onions and cover with foil.
4. Bake for 30 minutes. Remove from the oven and sprinkle with Cheddar. Pop the casserole back in the oven and bake until cheese is melted.

Apron Strings

Families today are eating out more, and everyone seems to be scattered instead of gathering at the table. Meetings, sports, dance rehearsals, events, church, and work are leaving many supper tables empty, cold, and void. I think it's a shame because the family unit needs to gather around the table. Turn off the TV. Turn your phones on silent and put them in another room. Sit around the table, and look into the eyes of the ones you hold so dear. Relax and enjoy the blessing of family and fellowship at your supper table. Your family will grow closer and make bonds that will never be broken. Let's not sacrifice our family for the world to exploit. Linger at your supper table with your loves. Make it a priority.

STEWED SQUASH

One of the great things about summer is the abundance of fresh squash. When you put squash and onions together, you have an automatic winner.

4 tablespoons bacon grease
2 pounds yellow squash
1 large onion (diced)
Salt and black pepper to taste

1. In a stainless-steel skillet, heat bacon grease over medium-low heat.
2. Cut squash into circles. Add squash to grease in skillet. Add onions on top of squash. Add salt and pepper to taste.

Cover with a lid. Cook over medium-low heat until squash is tender. Uncover and, using a spatula, cut squash and stir to combine with onions. Cook over medium heat until the squash juices have partly cooked out and squash is very tender, stirring the bottom of the skillet with a spatula.

Dallas and Isabella

Hannah at the stove

KITCHEN WISDOM

If you're buying squash at the market, remember that the smaller, light-yellow ones are usually more tender and cook down better than larger, dark-yellow squash.

SQUASH PATTIES

If you are lucky enough to have leftover Stewed Squash (page 35), you absolutely must use it to make Squash Patties. If not, boil some squash and use it to make this dish— even kids will eat squash when it's fried up!

⅓ cup vegetable oil
1½ cups leftover Stewed Squash (page 35) or 1½ cups boiled squash (drained well)
1 large egg (beaten)
⅔ cup White Lily self-rising flour
1 small onion (finely diced)
½ teaspoon black pepper
Salt to taste

1. In a skillet, heat oil over medium-low heat.
2. Mix all remaining ingredients together. Scoop out about 1 tablespoon squash mixture at a time and pat out flat in the skillet. Fry over medium-low heat until brown, about 1 minute. Turn patties to the other side to finish cooking. Remove and let drain on paper towels. Serve warm.

William and Big Daddy

Cape

GRANDBABIES' MEMORIES

Bay   When we were younger, Big Mama and Big Daddy took us on nature walks through the woods. We collected leaves, wildflowers, nuts, mushrooms, and anything else that caught our eye. We would sing and hold hands as we walked along the paths that Big Daddy had cut in the woods. When we arrived back to the house, we would all dump out our grocery store sacks that were full of all we had found on the kitchen table. We sat and looked through everything as Big Daddy told us about what each item was. He would tell what time of year each flower was in season, what animals might like to eat the different kinds of nuts and grass, and what berries were poisonous. When I think back on all the times shared around the kitchen table at Big Mama and Big Daddy's house, I remember Sunday lunches, late-night snacks, painting Christmas ornaments, many laughs, and cries. Yet, the one thing I remember the most fondly is looking at everything found on our nature walks, and the joy in Big Daddy's eyes as he told us about all we had found.

William   One day, Big Mama, Big Daddy, and I went to pick blueberries. While we were out picking, we decided to pick the squash and zucchini, too. When we got back home, Big Mama made Blueberry Delight. We ate it all up! It was so, so good!

Isabella   When thinking of Big Mama and her kitchen, one automatically imagines the table, or the stove, or even the chopping block, but I think of the sink. Not only have I had to wash dishes and clean veggies and fruits in the sink, but I have made memories. I can remember washing scrapes on my legs and arms when I fell in the yard or cleaning my hands before a meal. I remember when I attended Andalusia's homecoming dance, and Big Mama washed my hair in the kitchen sink. I do love the other parts of her kitchen, but the sink is where I have the most happy and funny memories.

Cape   My favorite memory in Big Mama's kitchen is sneaking in there late at night to eat a "midnight snack." We would all eat crackers with mayonnaise and ice cream. We would leave all the lights off and be extra quiet so we wouldn't wake up Big Mama and Big Daddy!

Banks   My favorite memory in the kitchen is making boxed mashed potatoes. Big Mama has never been the type to use boxed or preserved foods. One day, I was hungry, but she hadn't been to the grocery store. We went to the kitchen to see what was there, and all there was were some boxed mashed potatoes. I will always remember that even when Big Mama doesn't have her pantry stocked full, she's still gonna take care of her grandbabies, even if she has to make do with boxed mashed potatoes.

CHICKEN SOUP

The first time I ate this soup was at Jane and Leotis Garrett's home. I knew after the first bite I had to have the recipe. They lived on the river and fished all the time. The night we ate with them, they used fish instead of chicken. Cooking with what you have on hand (especially if it's fresh!) is always a good idea.

½   large onion (finely chopped)
1   clove garlic or ½ teaspoon minced garlic or ¼ teaspoon garlic powder
½   stick salted butter
2   cups chopped cooked chicken breast
2   cups chicken broth
1   (12-ounce) package processed cheese product (cubed)
2   (10.5-ounce) cans cream of chicken soup
1   (16-ounce) bag frozen whole kernel corn
1   (14.25-ounce) can cream-style corn
1   (10-ounce) can diced tomatoes with green chiles

1. In a large pot, cook onion, garlic, and butter over medium heat until vegetables are tender.
2. Add remaining ingredients. Cook for 30 minutes, stirring frequently.

THE FULL SOUL LOATHETH A HONEYCOMB; BUT TO THE HUNGRY SOUL EVERY BITTER THING IS SWEET.
—PROVERBS 27:7, KJV

Enjoying dinner with Walt, Hannah, Cape, Banks, and Bay

KITCHEN WISDOM

You can use fish, shrimp, or turkey in the place of chicken.

SAUSAGE-BEEF ENCHILADAS

This dish is so good, it will make you want to stand up and dance!

½ pound ground sausage
½ pound ground beef
½ large onion (chopped)
1 (10.5-ounce) can cream of mushroom soup
1 (10.75-ounce) can tomato soup
1 (10-ounce) can red enchilada sauce
1 (8-count) package 6-inch flour tortillas
3 cups grated Cheddar cheese
Refried beans
Sour cream

1. Preheat oven to 350°.
2. In a cast-iron skillet, cook ground sausage and beef over medium heat until browned. Drain well. Add onion to meat mixture and cook until softened.
3. In a saucepan, mix mushroom soup, tomato soup, and enchilada sauce together. Cook over medium heat until hot. Pour 1 cup soup mixture over meat mixture and stir to combine.
4. Spoon ¼ cup meat mixture onto each tortilla and top with 1 or 2 tablespoons cheese. Roll and place seam side down into the casserole dish. Pour remaining soup mixture over tortillas and sprinkle with remaining cheese.
5. Bake until hot and bubbly, about 30 minutes. Serve with refried beans and sour cream.

I WILL SING OF THE MERCIES OF THE LORD FOR EVER: WITH MY MOUTH WILL I

MAKE KNOWN THY FAITHFULNESS TO ALL GENERATIONS.

—PSALM 89:1, KJV

PARKING SPACE

As a family, we all have a certain seat at the table. I guess you'd say that is our parking space. We always look forward to the time of day when we gather with a good hot meal and exciting conversation. It makes folks feel special to know they have their own seat at the table. After George passed, we all had a hard time sitting in his seat. Hannah sits there now, but she had a lot of emotions about it for a long time. Each place at the table holds importance for other family members.

chapter 2

COMPANY'S COMING

MAMA'S ALWAYS RIGHT

My mama taught me well, and I listened well. This was her advice to me: Brenda, when you are expecting overnight company or just friends over for supper, always do these things a few days BEFORE the company arrives.

1. Set the table beautifully.
2. Make the salad, dessert, and tea.
3. Cut greenery and flowers from the yard. Do not buy them.
4. Tidy up the house. (Notice she didn't say clean the house. That's because her house was already clean.)
5. Put clean sheets on the beds where the guests will be sleeping. Make sure to put a sprig of greenery or a single flower in their room.

Mama gave me these tips so that it would free me up for a good visit with my guests, whether family or friends, whether overnighters or just coming for a meal. It was freeing me from working and allowing me to do what was important, visiting with them. All the friends that come to visit always say they feel at home at my house. That's exactly how I want them to feel. I want to have quality time with them.

I remember one time Mama and Daddy invited a soldier to our house for supper. Thinking that he would probably love some good, hot homemade biscuits, she made a huge pan of them. We were all seated at the dining room table—Daddy, Mama, my three brothers, me, and the soldier. She had fixed lots of delicious dishes for him. The soldier said, "These are the best biscuits I've ever had."

I quickly said, "You must like them. You have already eaten nine!" Oh my. My mama wanted to slide under the table. She was so embarrassed and probably wanted to spank me good right then and there. I guess I was probably in 7th grade with a hormone imbalance. WHAT WAS I THINKING?! Kids say the darndest things. Mama never let me forget that night. The soldier probably had heard worse and brushed it off.

Y'all know what scripture says. Use your blessings to honor God by sharing your blessings with others. Folks, your home is a blessing from God, and it is meant to be shared. God never said that everything had to be clean and perfect before you shared. It doesn't matter if the house is small or large. If it's bright and shiny clean or a little dusty like mine, it's still to be a home that welcomes guests.

Take the story of Mary and Martha in scripture. Mary sat at the feet of Jesus just visiting and loving on Jesus while Martha was in the kitchen complaining to Jesus about Mary not helping her prepare the meal. Jesus said, "Martha, you are worried and upset about many things, but only one thing is needed. Mary has chosen what is better, and it will not be taken away from her."

I think my mama had the right idea. She was doing what Jesus said. Mama prepared before the guests arrived so that she could give quality time to them. The ones living in the house with you also need your attention and special treatment.

The recipes in this chapter are just a few of the make-ahead dishes that will free you up to have a great visit with friends and family.

Lordy, Here They Come
2022
By Harti

MEMAMA'S PARTY ROLLS

There's nothing better than a buttered yeast roll on the tip of your tongue. You can't stop with just one! This is one of Bay's favorite things—she just loves bread!

½ cup sugar
¾ cup solid grease
1 cup whole buttermilk
1 teaspoon salt
¾ cup water
½ cup instant mashed potatoes
2 (0.25-ounce) packages active dry yeast
¼ cup warm water (105° to 110°)
2 large eggs
6 cups sifted White Lily all-purpose flour, divided

1. In a saucepan, heat sugar, solid grease, buttermilk, and salt over medium heat until grease melts. Remove from heat and add ¾ cup water. Add potatoes and mix with a wire whisk. Let cool until lukewarm.
2. Dissolve yeast in ¼ cup warm water.
3. Using a mixer, combine buttermilk mixture, eggs, and 3 cups flour. Add yeast mixture and beat at medium speed with dough hook until smooth. Add remaining 3 cups flour, a little at a time, and beat for 7 minutes.
4. Place dough in an oiled bowl, turning dough so that both sides of dough are greased. Store in refrigerator lightly covered until dough is doubled in size. (I leave mine overnight.) The dough will keep for a week.
5. Grease 2 (12-well) muffin pans. Pinch off a small amount of dough (about the size of a walnut) and roll into a ball. Place 3 balls of dough in each well of pans (like a cloverleaf). Let dough rise, uncovered, in pans in a warm place with no drafts for 2 hours.
6. Preheat oven to 425°.
7. Bake for 6 minutes. I slather mine with butter as soon as they come out of the oven—hot and delicious!

BE YE KIND ONE TO ANOTHER, TENDERHEARTED, FORGIVING ONE ANOTHER, EVEN AS GOD FOR CHRIST'S SAKE HATH FORGIVEN YOU.
—EPHESIANS 4:32, KJV

SPAGHETTI SAUCE

When I make this, I make the entire potful. I'm always hoping there will be leftovers to freeze for another day. But, when company comes, they usually lick the plate clean!

3 pounds ground beef
2 large onions (diced)
1 (4.5-ounce) jar sliced mushrooms (drained)
1 green bell pepper (diced)
4 (15-ounce) cans tomato sauce
1 (28-ounce) can diced tomatoes (undrained)
3 tablespoons dried Italian seasoning
2 tablespoons dried oregano
2 tablespoons garlic powder
2 teaspoons salt
Hot cooked spaghetti noodles
Grated Parmesan cheese

1. In a cast-iron skillet, brown ground beef. Drain off grease and transfer beef into a large stainless-steel boiler.
2. In the same skillet, sauté onions, mushrooms, and bell pepper until tender. Add vegetable mixture to beef in boiler. To boiler, add tomato sauce, tomatoes, Italian seasoning, oregano, garlic powder, and salt. Cook over medium-low heat for at least 30 minutes. Reduce heat to low and simmer until the flavors have blended, 1 to 2 hours. Serve over cooked spaghetti noodles and top with Parmesan.

KITCHEN WISDOM

Make this recipe your own. Some people like ground chuck, but I like hamburger meat better because I like the flavor of the fat in it. Some folks don't like mushrooms—if you don't, just leave them out! You can always experiment with adding different ingredients and flavors.

HANNAH'S CHICKEN SALAD

I do love a good ole chicken salad. I don't know a living soul who would turn it down! This recipe makes a smooth chicken salad—it's perfect for sandwiches and snacks when company is coming. I suggest making a lot—it won't last long!

4   boneless skinless chicken breasts
      (about 2½ pounds)
3 to 4 celery ribs, strings removed and
      finely chopped (about 1 cup)
2   cups mayonnaise
¼   cup sugar
½   teaspoon salt
½   teaspoon black pepper
Croissants, leaf lettuce, and sliced
      tomatoes

1. Trim fat and gristle from chicken breasts.
2. In a large stockpot, cover chicken with water and boil until done, about 15 to 20 minutes. Let cool for a few minutes.
3. Place chicken in a food processor and pulse until chicken is finely chopped.
4. In a large bowl, combine chicken with celery, mayonnaise, sugar, salt, and pepper. Serve with croissants, leaf lettuce, and sliced tomatoes.

At left: Bay, Cape, and Mary Caton play dress-ups
At right, clockwise: Cape, Bay, Banks, Hannah, and Brenda

KITCHEN WISDOM

Save your broth after you've cooked your chicken—you've got homemade chicken broth now! Think about all the ways you can use it! Or, if you don't have time to boil the chicken breasts, buy a rotisserie chicken from the grocery store and save yourself a step.

MACARONI SALAD

This is a very colorful dish with so many good ingredients in it! Dallas and I like to swing on the porch and eat a bowlful.

1 (16-ounce) package elbow macaroni (cooked according to package directions and cooled)
4 medium carrots (chopped and lightly boiled until crisp-tender)
3 celery ribs (chopped)
1 red bell pepper (chopped)
1 green bell pepper (chopped)
1 (6-ounce) container cherry tomatoes (leave whole)

6 green onions (chopped)
1 (4-ounce) jar diced pimentos (drained)
2 cups mayonnaise
Salt and black pepper to taste

1. Mix all ingredients together, folding until the mayonnaise is evenly distributed. Chill in refrigerator until ready to serve.

KITCHEN WISDOM

If I have leftover ham, I cube it into small pieces and add it. I can make a whole meal off this salad with a sleeve of round, buttery crackers and a glass of tea!

LONG TIME, NO SEE

Your dear old friends want the same things as you do! One thing they may wish for is to reconnect. You can be apart for 40 years and reconnect with good friends within two minutes of seeing them again. It's almost like you've never even been apart at all!

Most high school graduates try to have a class reunion every five years or so. Young men have no problem with this—you just grab your favorite faded jeans, a Hawaiian shirt, and tennis shoes, and you're ready to party. But, oh Lordy, with us women, it's a completely different story. We have to know at least a month before the reunion. Glory! Where do we start? We need to lose 10 pounds, wax our brows, get pedicures and manicures, color our hair and get it trimmed. Spray tan—well, maybe? What do we wear? This calls for a shopping trip! Hope those long, full blouses are still in style at reunion time—they cover a multitude of sins. Need to find new shoes and earrings to match the outfit. Hey girls, we need not worry about all that stuff! Just do like our men folks—wear a smile and be full of hugs, kisses, laughs, and stories to share.

It's extremely important to stay connected to folks. When my husband, George, passed away, my family and friends became lifesavers. My college girlfriends and I started traveling on adventure trips. My Andalusia, Alabama, girlfriends and I eat together and go on day trips, too. Someone in each group needs to be the planner. The others just show up and do what the planner says. I love it that way. I don't have to think—just show up and play my part of the adventure. Who could ask for more?

On one of my college girlfriend adventures, we rented a van, and five of us headed out from Alabama to East Texas. What a time we had! Just picture five 70-year-old ladies crawling in and out of a van. Someone should have taken a video of us. They could have made a million off the sales. We laughed at each other continually. I was the only smart one in the van because I knew to sit in the very back seat where all the yummy snacks were.

Two of my Andalusia friends and I went on a river kayaking adventure. When we checked in, the lady said the river was extremely dangerous because of all the rain they had. She said we probably would be fine since we were experienced kayakers. Little did she know that I had never even sat in a kayak. The other two just looked at each other, eyeball to eyeball with doubt if they should let me even attempt a fast moving river since I didn't have any experience at all. I quickly told them that I was going to kayak no matter what! Julie and I did great—but Pam, well, the current pushed her under every tree limb that was hanging over the river. She got a full workout that day. Julie and I just stayed right in the middle of the river like pros. With our appetite worked up, we stopped at a small out-of-the way restaurant and ate our fill. What a great day we had!

EDRA'S CONGEALED SALAD

I never went to my mother-in-law's house when she didn't have some kind of Jell-O with fruit cocktail in it, and it always had a whipped topping! This recipe is different than others, and the finished product looks impressive. It can be made several days before your company arrives.

1   (3-ounce) box lime gelatin
1   (3-ounce) box lemon gelatin
1½ cups hot water
1   (16-ounce) container cottage cheese
1   (20-ounce) can crushed pineapple (drain well)
1   cup mayonnaise
½   lemon (juiced)

½   teaspoon prepared horseradish
1   cup pecans (chopped)

1. In a large bowl, dissolve lime and lemon gelatins in 1½ cups hot water. Add remaining ingredients and stir, making sure to mix thoroughly. Spoon mixture into a gelatin mold or glass dish and refrigerate until firm.

CHICKEN VEGETABLE SOUP

This soup reminds me of my mama and daddy. We always had a big garden in Pickens County, Alabama. That's where we picked all the fresh vegetables for our pot of soup. You can use fresh or frozen produce in this recipe.

1 whole chicken (about 4 pounds)
1 (16-ounce) package frozen baby green lima beans
2 large onions (chopped)
1 (28-ounce) can diced tomatoes
3 cloves garlic (chopped)
½ head cabbage (chopped)
Salt and black pepper to taste
1 (16-ounce) package frozen sliced okra
1 (16-ounce) package frozen white creamed corn
MeMama's Cornbread Muffins (recipe on page 131)

1. In a large stockpot, add chicken and enough water to slightly cover the chicken. Bring to a boil over medium heat and cook until chicken is tender. Remove chicken and reserve the broth in the pot. Shred chicken, discarding skin and bones, and set aside.

2. To the broth in pot, add lima beans, onions, tomatoes, garlic, and cabbage. Add salt and pepper to taste. Cook over medium heat until lima beans are tender. Add okra; bring to a boil and cook for 5 minutes. Reduce heat to low and simmer. Add corn and chicken; cook for 10 minutes. Serve with MeMama's Cornbread Muffins.

Brenda reading a book about gardening

KITCHEN WISDOM

This is a great soup when you don't know what time your company is coming. Just keep it on the stove and heat it back up when they arrive. It freezes well, too.

HAWAIIAN BANANA-NUT BREAD

You can serve this bread to your company for breakfast or with afternoon coffee. I like it fresh out of the oven. Actually, everyone loves it!

3 cups White Lily all-purpose flour
¾ teaspoon salt
1 teaspoon baking soda
2 cups sugar
1 teaspoon ground cinnamon
1 cup chopped pecans or walnuts
3 large eggs, beaten
1 cup vegetable oil
2 cups mashed ripe bananas
1 (8-ounce) can crushed pineapple (drained)
2 teaspoons vanilla extract

1. Preheat oven to 350°. Grease and flour 2 (8½x4½-inch) loaf pans.
2. In a large bowl, combine flour, salt, baking soda, sugar, and cinnamon; stir in pecans.
3. In another large bowl, combine eggs, oil, bananas, pineapple, and vanilla. Add banana mixture to flour mixture, stirring just until dry ingredients are moistened.

Spoon batter into prepared pans.
4. Bake until a wooden pick inserted in center comes out clean, 1 hour and 10 minutes. Let cool in pans for 10 minutes. Remove from pans and let cool on wire racks.

William and Isabella doing dishes in Big Mama's kitchen

KITCHEN WISDOM

This recipe makes two loaves. You can use this same recipe but substitute zucchini to make Zucchini Nut Bread or use carrots for Carrot Nut Bread. That's three recipes in one—can't beat that!

BLUEBERRY FRENCH TOAST

This dish is "fancy, dancy, and delicious!" Your company will think they are at a five-star hotel when breakfast is served. If you're planning to host a brunch, serve this. It can be made a day ahead, then you can just pop it in the oven when you're ready to make sure it's good and hot.

1   (16-ounce) loaf Italian bread (cubed)
1   cup whole milk
1   cup half-and-half
12 large eggs
⅓   cup maple syrup
1   teaspoon vanilla extract
2   (8-ounce) packages cream cheese (softened)
1   cup fresh blueberries
Blueberry Sauce

1. Preheat oven to 350°.
2. Layer cubed Italian bread in a 14x11-inch casserole dish.
3. In a large bowl, whisk together milk, half-and-half, eggs, syrup, and vanilla. Pinch off small pieces of cream cheese and add to milk mixture.

4. Sprinkle blueberries evenly over bread. Pour milk mixture over bread, making sure each piece is covered and cream cheese is evenly distributed.
5. Cover and bake for 30 minutes. Uncover and bake for 25 to 30 minutes more. Pour warm Blueberry Sauce over the top and enjoy!

BLUEBERRY SAUCE

1   cup sugar
2   tablespoons cornstarch
1   cup water
1   tablespoon salted butter
1   cup blueberries (frozen or fresh)

1. In a saucepan, mix together sugar and cornstarch. Gradually add 1 cup water, stirring constantly. Add butter and bring to a low boil over medium-low heat. Add blueberries, stirring to combine.

Apron Strings

Remember, the dishes, lawn, and housework aren't going anywhere. So, get with your friends, laugh, talk, eat, and enjoy one another. You will be blessed for doing so, and they will be refreshed and happy. You don't have to cook much for your company. A nice pot of soup and cornbread is all that's needed.

CINNAMON ROLLS

Everybody will feel special if you go to the trouble of making these. Serve these warm to your company for a cozy breakfast on a cold day. Walt never turns down Cinnamon Rolls.

⅔ cup sugar
2 tablespoons ground cinnamon
Memama's Party Rolls dough (recipe on
 page 49)
1½ sticks melted salted butter, divided
Cream Cheese Glaze

1. In a small bowl, mix sugar and cinnamon together and set aside.
2. On a lightly floured surface, roll out the dough to a little over ¼ inch thickness. Smear half of the melted butter on top of dough. Sprinkle cinnamon-sugar mixture over dough. Cut dough in 10x1-inch strips and roll up each strip into a cinnamon roll shape.
3. Grease a 14x11-inch casserole dish with butter. Place rolls in the dish with sides touching. Pour remaining butter over rolls. Let rolls rise, uncovered, in dish in a warm place with no drafts for 1 hour and 30 minutes to 2 hours.
4. Preheat oven to 350°. Bake for 30 minutes or less. Spread Cream Cheese Glaze over hot rolls.

IF POSSIBLE, SO FAR AS IT
DEPENDS ON YOU, LIVE
PEACEABLY WITH ALL.
—ROMANS 12:18, ESV

CREAM CHEESE GLAZE

1 (8-ounce) package cream cheese
 (softened)
1 stick salted butter (melted)
4 tablespoons whole milk
1 teaspoon vanilla extract
2 cups powdered sugar

1. Mix cream cheese and butter together. Add milk and vanilla; beat with a mixer at medium speed. Add powdered sugar, beating well.

Walt and Brenda

BEEF STEW

Sometimes, chuck roast can be expensive, but remember—you can feed a lot of people with it! I like to make this for Sunday dinner. When we get back from church, we can just sit down and eat without waiting.

1   (3-pound) chuck roast (cut into ½-inch cubes)
Salt and black pepper to taste
10   carrots (sliced into ½-inch circles)
2   large onions (diced)
2   (28-ounce) cans diced tomatoes
3   garlic cloves (minced)
8   russet potatoes (peeled and cut into ½-inch cubes)

1. In a large stockpot with lid, bring roast and water to cover to a boil over medium-high heat. (You start with the meat because you want the flavors of the meat to come out and make a broth.) Reduce heat to medium. Add salt and pepper to taste. Cover and cook for 30 minutes. Add carrots, onions, tomatoes, and garlic. Cook for 30 minutes. Add potatoes and cook until tender.

KITCHEN WISDOM

Be sure to use a sharp knife when cutting the beef. You can also find the beef already cut for you. When the potatoes have cooked for a while and are tender, you can go ahead and enjoy a bowl of stew. But, I like to simmer my stew for another hour or so to make sure all the meat is tender and the flavors have blended together. I like to eat my Beef Stew with cornbread or crackers.

THE SWAYING BUS

The huge tour bus pulled up on the side of the road right in front of my humble home, which is in the middle of nowhere. My friends, Carole Henry, Andrea Holmes, Brenda Justiss, and I were dressed in our finest dressy casuals with makeup and the works. Mark Lowry, a famous gospel singer, had invited us to ride in his new tour bus to Ozark, Alabama. We were as excited as could be! Going on a tour bus with a famous person was a once-in-a-lifetime experience for us. We packed snacks, dips, chips, cake, sandwiches, and veggies for the ride—and a hungry appetite!

When we arrived, there were no places to eat nearby. Talk about starving—we were! So, we pulled out all the goodies and displayed them on a table in the bus. We ate until our hearts' content. We joked with

Mark Lowry, Brenda, and Andrew Greer

Mark about not even buying us supper! Good thing we gals carried vittles along. After the wonderful concert by Mark, we headed back home. The bus was rocking from side to side in the wind. I got sicker and sicker until my stomach began to roll. I thought I would never get back home to solid ground! When we finally got back to my house that night, I was the first one off the bus. I walked up my driveway in the dark and never looked back. I went and got straight into bed without even saying goodbye to my friends or Mark! I had no idea when they left, and I didn't even care!

I think all of our life experiences teach us a thing or two. I learned that night I don't want to ever ride on a tour bus again! Never! Next time, I'll just follow along behind in my favorite old Ford pickup truck!

Don't worry, Mark has come back to visit me again. Last time, he brought his friend Andrew Greer with him. We spent time in my kitchen, and they recorded us for their video podcast, called *Dinner Conversations*. Lordy, the things I've gotten to do and stories I've now got to tell—my younger self might never have believed it!

ALABAMA FIRECRACKERS

This is one of William's favorites. He puts a whole cracker in his mouth with one bite. They're a great make-ahead for company, tailgating, and parties!

1   cup canola oil or olive oil
3   tablespoons or 1 (1-ounce) package ranch dressing mix
2   tablespoons crushed red pepper
1   teaspoon garlic powder
1   teaspoon onion powder
¼   teaspoon ground red pepper
1   package unsalted saltine crackers (all 4 sleeves)

1. Preheat oven to 350°.
2. Mix together oil, ranch dressing mix, crushed red pepper, garlic powder, onion powder, and ground red pepper.
3. Place crackers in a roasting pan. Evenly pour oil mixture over the crackers, gently stirring.
4. Bake for 25 minutes. Gently stir crackers after 15 minutes so that oil mixture is distributed over each cracker. Let cool completely and store in a resealable plastic bag or sealed container.

A HOME FOR EVERYONE

Before Dallas and Hannah went to college, while they were just teenagers, our home was known as the place to come and get some good food. All the boys came with Dallas, and the girls came with Hannah. It's so important that you let your children bring their friends to your home. They don't care if it's clean or dirty. They just want to be together in someone's home. As long as you can fix them something to eat and wear a smile, they are happy. Let your children's friends know that your house is open for them.

Hannah's girlfriends loved to come over often. One night, George and I were in bed, and I heard someone tapping on Hannah's window. I wondered who in the world that could be at this hour. So, I got up to see, and it was one of Hannah's girlfriends. "Can I spend the night here tonight?" she asked. I told her that Hannah wasn't home yet, but she was welcome to stay. She came to the door, walked in, and went straight to bed.

Another time, Hannah wanted to roll yards at Homecoming. This was a tradition in our little town and still is today. During Homecoming week, the kids would take toilet paper and roll the trees in other people's yards. I told her she wasn't going to do that. She was insistent that they do something. So, I said, "I tell ya what, you go over there to Pawpaw's cow pasture, get you a bunch of cow patties, and take them around to put in people's yards. It will be excellent fertilizer." Hannah and four or five girls got shovels and went over to Pawpaw's in my pickup truck and loaded it up. About dark-thirty, they went out and emptied that whole truckload of manure around Andalusia and just had the best time. I wanted to go, too! But George said, "You can't go, Brenda; you're an adult. You'll be arrested!" When they got home, they were so filthy and smelly that I made them wash off outside! I think Andalusia grass is still the greenest grass around!

Another time, George had cooked a huge deer leg all night long on the smoker. He brought it in the house and sat it on the table. It wasn't a mealtime, but Hannah and her friends came and sat around the table talking. They got a knife and started hacking off pieces off that leg, and before we knew it, half of that deer leg was gone. Those girls had the best time sitting together around that table.

Dallas's friends, well, you better have a big pot of something to eat if they were coming. Teenage boys are never full. They can eat you out of house and home. Sometimes, Dallas would have them all over to spend the night. They always slept in the den on the floor, in lounge chairs, or on the couch.

George and I always enjoyed being around our children's friends. We bonded with them, too. Even today, when I see one of the kids (now full-grown adults), I think back to the good times we all had at our home.

CARROT CAKE

—◆—

Have you ever noticed that there is no room in the refrigerator when company's coming? This Carrot Cake is the perfect dessert to fix when you have folks coming. You can make it ahead of time and don't need to refrigerate it. This is one of Banks's favorite desserts—she loves it!

3   cups White Lily all-purpose flour
1   tablespoon baking soda
1   teaspoon salt
1   tablespoon ground cinnamon
1½ cups sugar
1½ cups corn oil
4   large eggs
1   tablespoon vanilla extract
¾   cup crushed pineapple (drained well)
¾   cup sweetened flaked coconut
1⅓ cups grated carrots
1½ cups chopped pecans
Cream Cheese Icing
Chopped toasted pecans (for topping)

1. Preheat oven to 350°.
2. In a large bowl, mix together flour, baking soda, salt, and cinnamon. Set aside.
3. In a large bowl, mix together sugar, oil, eggs, and vanilla. Slowly add flour mixture to sugar mixture, stirring to combine. Add pineapple, coconut, and carrots, mixing together. Add pecans.

4. Pour batter into 3 (9-inch) round greased and floured cake pans. Bake until cakes pull away from the pans, 25 to 30 minutes. Let cool in pans. Remove and let cool completely on wire racks.
5. Once cake layers have cooled, spread Cream Cheese Icing between layers, adding a sprinkle of pecans between each layer. Finish by icing top and sides of cake. Top with toasted pecans.

CREAM CHEESE ICING

3   (8-ounce) blocks cream cheese (room temperature)
1½ sticks salted butter (room temperature)
¾   cup firmly packed light brown sugar
1½ teaspoons ground cinnamon
1   cup powdered sugar

1. Beat all ingredients together with a mixer at medium speed until creamy. Use immediately.

KITCHEN WISDOM

To make grating and chopping your carrots easier, you can use a food processor. Sometimes, I don't like to dirty up another gadget, but it can be handy!

❧〜❧

chapter 3

O HOLY NIGHT

CHRISTMAS MEMORY

My bedroom window faced the front yard of our house. Mama had put me to bed early on this particular Christmas Eve night because I was sick with fever. I tossed and turned in my bed thinking about Santa coming and wondering if he would pass over our house because I wasn't asleep yet. I began to try harder to go to sleep, and after a while, I finally drifted off.

When I was sound asleep, I began to hear banging, talking, and other noises coming from the front lawn that woke me up. While staying in bed, I peeked out the windows through the thin curtains and blinds. Was it Santa Claus? No. There was Mama and Daddy lugging in shiny new bikes for my brothers and me.

On that memorable night, I realized for the first time that there was no Santa Claus! I cried!

My childhood wonder has long passed me now, and Jesus is my wonder, my noise in the night. He is the one I look to, the one who gives joy and amazement, bearing gifts of eternal life, joy, contentment, daily bread, family, peace, healing, and His holy word, the Bible. He gives us the choice of receiving the gifts, never forcing any gift upon anyone, but offering His gifts to everyone that wants to receive.

Bay, Cape, Big Mama, William, Isabella, and Banks

The Savior Is Born
2022
B. Gantt

Jesus left his throne in heaven to come to this sinful earth as a baby. He came to offer the gift of forgiveness and the gift of eternal life with Him to all those who would receive.

Christmas is a special time to celebrate our Savior's birth. Our family always gets together at Christmas to celebrate. We, too, give gifts of love to one another just as our Lord set the example.

Jesus said, "It is more blessed to give than to receive." He gave his life for you and me—we live our life for Him.

Merry Christmas, Jesus.

DECORATING FOR THE HOLIDAYS

The beauty and smell of fresh cedar, pine boughs, holly, and winter shrubs are in almost every room in my home. My Christmas tree holds a few bought ornaments, but most were made by my children and grandchildren when they were young. Getting out my decorations every year brings back so many memories.

FRUITCAKE

———◆———

I can see it now—this cake sitting like a queen under that cake dome at my mama's house on Christmas Eve. It's packed full of goodies. Christmas just isn't Christmas without Fruitcake and coffee.

1 cup sugar
4 large eggs (room temperature)
2 cups White Lily all-purpose flour
4 teaspoons baking powder
½ teaspoon salt
1 tablespoon pumpkin pie spice
1 pound candied red cherries (whole)
1 pound candied green cherries (whole)
1 pound candied pineapple (green and red if you can find it; yellow candied if you can't)
1 pound candied dates (chopped)
2 quarts pecan halves
Puerto Rican rum or bourbon

3. In a bowl, sift together flour, baking powder, salt, and pie spice. Add cherries, pineapple, and dates to flour mixture. With your hands, toss all the fruit to coat with flour mixture. Add pecans and toss to coat. Add sugar mixture to fruit mixture, stirring well with a large spoon.

4. Grease and flour a tube pan (do not use a Bundt pan). Spread the batter into the prepared pan. Make sure it is packed very hard in the pan using the back of a spoon.

5. Bake for 2 hours. Let cool completely in the pan for about 5 hours. Remove cake from pan. Brush the sides and top of cake with rum or bourbon. Sprinkle rum on a large square of cheesecloth and wrap it around the cake. Leave the cloth on the cake until it is ready to serve.

1. Preheat oven to 275°.
2. Beat sugar and eggs together with a mixer at medium speed and set aside.

Apron Strings

This was my Mama's recipe, and I've eaten it all my life. When I was making this for the first time recently, I realized I had a few questions. I wanted to call her and talk to her about them, but I realized I couldn't because she's in heaven. Make sure you talk to your loved ones about how to make their recipes. Those recipes will be a comfort to you when your loves are gone.

KITCHEN WISDOM

The important things to remember are to pack the batter as hard as you can into the tube pan and let it cool completely, at least 5 hours or more. Also, this cake can NEVER be cooked in a Bundt pan. You will not be able to get it out.

SPICED TEA

Wrap your hand around a warm cup of Spiced Tea and take a sip. All your burdens will melt away.

4 cups water
1 family-size tea bag or 5 regular tea bags
17 whole cloves
4 cinnamon sticks
1 cup pineapple juice
1¾ cups orange juice
¼ cup lemon juice (fresh squeezed)
1½ to 2 cups sugar (depending on your taste)
2 to 3 quarts extra water (depending on how strong you prefer the tea)

1. In a large pot, heat 4 cups water over medium-high heat until almost to a boil. Add tea bag, pushing bag down in the water. Cover with lid and set aside for 10 minutes.
2. Remove the tea bag, squeezing it to get out all the goodies!
3. Add cloves and cinnamon sticks. Pour in all the juices. Add sugar and extra water, stirring well.
4. Simmer over medium-low heat until the spices integrate into the tea, about 1 hour. Discard cloves and cinnamon sticks. Serve hot.

Brenda and Hannah love Spiced Tea at Christmas

My son, keep thy father's commandments, and forsake not the law of thy mother. Bind them continually upon thine heart, and tie them about thy neck.
—Proverbs 6:20–21, KJV

This vintage Christmas tin belonged to George's mama. I picked it for mine when she passed away. I enjoy using it and looking at the peaceful scene on it.

SNACK MIXES

We all like something we can munch on. The only trouble is—once you start munching on these snack mixes, you won't be able to stop! We always make these mixes for the holidays because we are big munchers in this family!

DILL SNACK MIX

3 cups crispy rice cereal squares
3 cups crispy wheat cereal squares
3 cups crispy corn cereal squares
3 cups oyster crackers
3 cups small twisted pretzels
3 cups white cheddar cheese crackers
3 cups pecan halves
2 cups vegetable oil
6 tablespoons dried dill
6 tablespoons dry ranch dressing mix

1. Preheat oven to 250°.
2. Place cereals, crackers, pretzels, and pecans in a roasting pan.
3. In a medium bowl, whisk together vegetable oil, dill, and ranch dressing mix. Pour dill mixture slowly over cereal mixture, while stirring evenly to coat.
4. Bake until the nuts taste roasted, about 1 hour and 10 minutes, stirring well every 10 to 15 minutes.

GARLIC SNACK MIX

3 cups Cheddar cheese cracker squares
3 cups oyster crackers
3 cups crispy rice cereal squares
3 cups crispy wheat cereal squares
3 cups crispy corn cereal squares
3 cups small twisted pretzels
3 cups pecans or mixed nuts
2 sticks salted butter
2 tablespoons garlic powder
3 tablespoons Worcestershire sauce
2 teaspoons hot sauce
2 teaspoon onion powder
3 teaspoons seasoned salt

1. Preheat oven to 250°.
2. Place crackers, cereals, pretzels, and pecans in a roasting pan.
3. In a saucepan, melt butter over medium heat. Stir in garlic powder, Worcestershire, hot sauce, onion powder, and seasoned salt. Pour butter mixture over the dry ingredients while stirring to cover the mixture fully.
4. Bake until the nuts taste roasted, about 1 hour to 1 hour and 10 minutes, stirring well every 10 to 15 minutes.

CHEESE RING

Isn't this a beautiful ring? That marmalade or jam makes it so festive and delicious. 'Tis the season for a special dish.

3 (8-ounce) packages cream cheese (softened)
2 cups sharp grated Cheddar cheese
1 cup chopped pecans (toasted)
1 teaspoon salted butter
1 jar orange marmalade or raspberry jam
Round buttery crackers

1. Beat cream cheese with a mixer at medium speed until creamy. Mix in Cheddar.
2. In a cast-iron skillet, cook pecans and butter over medium-low heat, stirring often, until pecans are crispy and toasted.
3. Form cheese mixture into a ring on a pretty, round plate. Flatten the top of the ring with a knife. Top the ring with marmalade or jam. Sprinkle with toasted pecans. Serve with round buttery crackers.

Bay, Isabella, Cape, and William singing Christmas carols around our outdoor Christmas tree

THE VILLAIN

Dallas and Hannah made this special T-shirt for their daddy for Christmas. Their eyes were open wide waiting for him to tear the present open. George was always having to say, "No, you can't do that, Dallas," or "No, you can't go there, Hannah." So, as a result, he became known as the villain of the family. It's something how we remember certain gifts we get. This homemade T-shirt was so special to George—he wore it with pride just because his children made it. I bet lots of other homes have villains in their families, too!

SMALL-TOWN CHRISTMAS

In Andalusia, Alabama, the whole month of December is packed with Christmas activities for people young and old! Children with bright smiles dressed in green and red sing carols in our nursing homes and visit our elderly folks living at home. The First Baptist Church does a nighttime drive-through live Nativity scene, complete with camels, donkeys, and church members in period costumes. Our Chamber of Commerce celebrates by providing Candyland, a gigantic Christmas display in the town square and on nearby properties with ice-skating, a snow slide, huge Christmas trees, horse-drawn carriages, mini Christmas cottages, and lights galore. Each of the businesses decorates their shop windows and storefronts to spread the cheer and merriment of the season. We have an annual parade downtown, too. One year, I was asked to be one of the grand marshals and rode on a float with Banks and Cape, waving and smiling at all the folks we passed. At Bethany Baptist Church, where my family goes, we have a meaningful Christmas Eve candlelight service, where we take The Lord's Supper and then gather in a circle with our lit candles to sing "Silent Night." I'm so proud that our little town celebrates Jesus's birth with joyful noises, loving spirits, and giving hearts.

AMBROSIA

The smell of fresh-peeled oranges lets me know it's Christmastime for sure! My recipe for this Southern dish is pretty simple, but you can add cherries or nuts, too. Make it the night before so that it will be ready when your company arrives.

12 fresh, juicy oranges
1 fresh coconut (can also use preshredded coconut)
⅓ cup sugar

1. Over a bowl, peel and cut oranges, allowing the juices to drip down into the bowl.
2. For coconut, poke holes in each of the 3 eyes using an ice pick or sharp knife.

Turn the coconut upside down over a glass and let the coconut milk pour out.
3. Take the coconut outside and hit it with a hammer to crack open. Remove the outer shell and peel it. Then, grate the white meat into fine shreds.
4. Mix coconut, oranges, and sugar together. Refrigerate.

Apron Strings

Ambrosia brings back a ton of memories of my childhood—the smell of fresh oranges radiating throughout the house, the sound of Daddy hitting the coconut with a hammer, the taste of the coconut milk, Mama letting me eat the pieces of coconut that were too small to hold to the grater. Precious memories—how they ever flood my soul! Be sure to include your children and grandchildren in the kitchen when you're cooking for holidays. They'll have memories to last a lifetime.

KITCHEN WISDOM

If you use fresh coconut, be sure to wear safety glasses while cracking the coconut. Go outside to do the cracking because those pieces can fly!

CHOCOLATE CHIP OATMEAL COOKIES

This recipe was my mother's, and my recipe card is beaten and battered from how much I've used it. If you pour me a cold glass of milk in a tin cup and give me a saucer of cookies, I'll be a happy camper.

1½   cups White Lily all-purpose flour (sifted)
1   teaspoon baking soda
1   teaspoon salt
1   cup solid shortening
¾   cup granulated sugar
¾   cup brown sugar
2   large eggs
1   teaspoon hot water
1   teaspoon vanilla extract
1½   cups chopped pecans
1   (12-ounce) package chocolate chips
2   cups old-fashioned oats

1. Preheat oven to 350°. Lightly grease a baking sheet.
2. Sift together flour, baking soda, and salt in a bowl.
3. Beat shortening with a mixer at medium speed until fluffy. Add sugars, beating well. Beat in eggs and 1 teaspoon hot water.
4. Add flour mixture to sugar mixture, beating until combined. Add vanilla and mix well. Fold in pecans, chocolate chips, and oats. Drop batter by tablespoonfuls on baking sheet.
5. Bake for 10 to 12 minutes.

KITCHEN WISDOM

You can make this batter at night and refrigerate it so that you can bake the cookies the next morning. Cook with your granchildren, and always lick the batter off the beater, spoon, and bowl!

BACK SEAT FLOORBOARD

Glory! When friends get together, the constant talking, belly-laughing, giving wise advice, and exchanging recipes never stop.

It was pouring down rain when Carole, Andrea, and I ran from The Cottle House to my truck. Andrea called out to Carole to get in the front seat of the truck with us—of course, Carole never listens to either of us. She crawled into the back behind the driver's seat.

The back seats were pushed up because all of our stuff was on the floorboard. There was no place for Carole. There was a small cardboard box sitting on the floorboard of the truck. Carole thought it was full of my recipe books and proceeded to sit on it like a stool. When she put her fanny on the box, it collapsed like a brick on a June bug. Carole fell flat on her butt in the back floorboard.

Andrea and I started laughing until we cried and almost wet our pants. Carole was hollering and laughing at the same time. Carole has had a hip replacement, so when she gets down, it takes an industrial crane to get her up. We told her to just lie there until we finished getting a china cabinet and putting it in the back of the truck. Remember when I

said it was pouring down rain? Like cats and dogs, it was!

Well, the truck was stuck. The tires were only halfway showing. By then, we were all hysterical with laughter! Nothing was going right for us. I told them to sit tight while I got out in the rain to search for boards to go under the tires. I pushed and pushed the boards under the tires, but the truck just got stuck deeper and deeper into the mud. I was looking like a wet, nasty dog by then, but I decided we would get home any way we could.

With a lot of effort, we finally got Carole up from the truck's floorboard, and we all started walking home in the rain. Carole found a dishpan that she put on the top of her head, Andrea giggled the whole way home, and me? Well, I had to completely strip down when we got back. Do y'all know how hard it is to take off wet jeans and boots? We were so nasty that we took off our clothes in the laundry room and put on housecoats and T-shirts. We proceeded to make a pot of coffee to warm our bodies, and we cut some fruitcake, too. We talked about the mess Carole got us into on that rainy, ugly day.

Just like the TV commercial that says, "I've fallen, and I can't get up," that's what happened to us. Good friends just laugh at their bloopers, and we will laugh for many years to come whenever we think back on that day that Carole wouldn't listen to us.

BREAD DOUGH ORNAMENTS

*Get your babies or your friends together and have a great time making these ornaments.
Don't forget to sign and date them on the back! They'll last for years with the sealent.*

2   cups White Lily all-purpose flour
2   cups salt
1   cup water
Assorted acrylic craft paints
Clear gloss acrylic spray sealer

1. Preheat oven to 300°.
2. Mix flour, salt, and 1 cup water together. If dough is too sticky, just sprinkle a little flour over dough and work it in.
3. Form the ornaments: snowmen, stars, manger, animals, Christmas trees. Just be creative!
4. Wet your fingertip and smooth out the surface of the ornaments. Make a whole in the top of each ornament with a toothpick. Don't make the hole too little, as the dough will expand some and may close up the hole.
5. Bake until very hard and dry. Let cool completely.
6. Once cooled, paint each ornament with acrylic craft paint. When the paint dries, spray front and back of ornaments with sealer to protect them from moisture. They will last for years and years!

MEMAMA'S CHEESE WAFERS

These wafers are spicy, and adults love them! I could eat all of them in one sitting! They're perfect for snacking when folks come over for holidays—Thanksgiving, Christmas, Fourth of July—they are a hit every time!

1 cup salted butter (room temperature)
2 (8-ounce) blocks sharp Cheddar cheese (grated with a box grater)
1 teaspoon dry mustard
1 teaspoon ground red pepper
1 cup White Lily all-purpose flour
¾ cup finely chopped pecans
2 cups crisp rice cereal

1. Preheat oven to 350°.
2. Mix butter and cheese until combined well. Add ground mustard and red pepper. Mix in flour, pecans, and cereal.
3. Roll mixture into 1-inch balls. Place on an ungreased baking sheet about 2 inches apart and press down with a fork in two directions.
4. Bake for 10 to 12 minutes.

UNLEAVENED BREAD
(LORD'S SUPPER)

The Communion table—Christians all over the world proclaim and remember Jesus with this special bread and drink. We examine ourselves, our faults, and our shortcomings before we partake of the supper. If we feel unworthy, we do not partake, but first admit and repent in our hearts. Then, we partake. One of the times our church offers the Lord's Supper is on Christmas Eve in remembrance of our risen savior, Jesus Christ.

⅓ cup olive oil
1 cup all-purpose White Lily flour
¼ teaspoon salt
⅓ cup water

1. Preheat oven to 400°.
2. Mix oil, flour, and salt together. Slowly add

⅓ cup water, working it into the flour mixture.
3. In an 8- or 10-inch greased skillet, spread the dough out very thin on the skillet with the tips of your greased fingers. Keep spreading until the dough is about the same thickness all over.
4. Bake until light brown, about 8 to 10 minutes.

COMMUNION

BY WALT MERRELL

Jesus lingered around many tables. He well understood that building relationships was an essential component of His ministry. Perhaps though, the most important table He lingered at was when He gave the disciples wine and bread at what is known as the Last Supper. Giving them wine to drink, He suggested the wine was representative of the blood He would spill for all of humanity, and the bread was representative of His body, offered as a living sacrifice for the atonement of sin. Encouraging the disciples, He suggested they should take wine and bread "in remembrance of me."

The taking of Communion is our remembrance of what Jesus did for us. When we take the wine (or grape juice in some churches), we simply do it as a reminder of the blood Jesus spilled for us when He was hung upon the cross. We eat a small wafer of unleavened bread also as a reminder that He gave of Himself so that we could be free from the bondage of sin.

You see, we cannot earn our way into heaven. We simply cannot be "good enough." I once heard it said that we should pile all of our "bad" deeds and thoughts to our right, and all of our "good" deeds and thoughts to our left, and see what happens. For all of us, the "bad" pile would far outgrow the "good" pile. That being the case, it should be obvious that none of us will ever be "good" enough to go to heaven. So, Jesus had to die on the cross.

He came to earth, fully man and fully the Son of God. God loves us so much that He sent Jesus to die on the cross, so that atonement . . . that is, the price to be paid . . . could be made for our sins. When Jesus died, He was the sacrifice for . . . He was the price paid . . . He accepted the punishment we deserved . . . so that we have the opportunity to come before God in heaven.

For you see, God will never be in the presence of sin. That said, without Jesus, sin would prevent us from ever entering heaven. But because of His sacrifice, our sins are "washed in the blood" as we like to say, and if we confess our sins and repent of our sinful ways and embrace God as our Father and Jesus as our Savior, then heaven's gates are open to us.

So why do we take Communion? Well . . . because He told us to, and because we all should be intentional to "remember" what He did for you . . . and for me.

God bless.

FOR AS OFTEN AS YOU EAT THIS BREAD AND DRINK THIS CUP, YOU PROCLAIM THE LORD'S DEATH UNTIL HE COMES.

—1 CORINTHIANS 11:26, ESV

UNCLE PICKENS'S PECANS

George and I loved Uncle Pickens and Aunt Evelyn, and they loved us and our children. Uncle Pickens lived just down the road from us. I would go visit, and we'd walk around the yard and pick up pecans as we strolled together. You see, he lived right in the middle of a pecan grove. The trees were huge. Uncle Pickens knew I loved pecans, so as we walked, he'd pick two of them up and crack them for me in his big, strong hands. I never was able to do that! He'd throw the shells on the ground and hand me the pecan halves. Boy, were they good! But the best part was the memories we made together—just an old man and a young married woman enjoying a good visit and special times together. The simple times in life are the very best times of all!

1 quart pecan halves
½ cup salt

1. In a bowl, combine pecans and salt and cover with water. Let stand for 30 minutes.
2. Take pecans out of water and spread them out on a baking sheet. Let dry for 2 hours.
3. Preheat oven to 250°.
4. Bake for 1 hour, stirring every 15 minutes.

Uncle Pickens

TABLES HAVE MANY USES

George's Uncle Pickens told us that boy and girl babies of yesteryears all wore cotton gowns. When a baby started crawling, the mother would pick up one leg of the table and place it on top of the tail of the child's gown to keep the child from crawling away. That way, the mother could get her work done. Uncle Pickens said his mama did that to him. He was a rambunctious child. The table we now have in our kitchen is the same table that held Pickens's gown under its leg so his mama could wash the supper dishes and keep him out of trouble.

DATE NUT BALLS

Not only do these taste delicious, but they are also a beautiful way to decorate your Christmas table, especially if you have a compote or pretty platter to put them on.

1 cup sugar
1 cup salted butter
1 (1-pound) package chopped dates
1 cup finely chopped pecans
2 cups crisp rice cereal
Powdered sugar

1. In a medium saucepan or skillet, cook sugar, butter, and dates over medium heat, stirring constantly, until mixture gets thick and butter is absorbed, about 10 minutes.

2. Remove pan from heat and add pecans, stirring to combine.

3. Place cereal in a large bowl. Pour date mixture over cereal and gently stir to combine. Let the mixture stand until cool to the touch.

4. Break off small globs and roll them into walnut-size balls using the palms of your hands.

5. Place powdered sugar in a lunch-size paper bag. Add a couple of balls at a time and shake gently. Get ready; it's gonna be good, y'all!

CHILDREN, OBEY YOUR PARENTS IN THE LORD: FOR THIS IS RIGHT. HONOUR THY FATHER AND MOTHER; WHICH IS THE FIRST COMMANDMENT WITH PROMISE; THAT IT MAY BE WELL WITH THEE, AND THOU MAYEST LIVE LONG ON THE EARTH.
—EPHESIANS 6:1–3, KJV

BAY

ISABELLA

CAPE

WILLIAM

BANKS

Every Christmas, each member of the family (children and adults) puts on a headdress, and we take pictures. We go into the woods and cut vines to make them, then we stick in greenery. Y'all should see the men of the family with theirs on!

Chapter 4

DESSERT AND COFFEE

IT'S ALL ABOUT TOGETHERNESS

My favorite desserts are warm pies and crunchy cookies. I enjoy them most when the pie is served with good hot coffee, and the cookies are served with a glass of ice-cold milk. If someone makes a homemade cobbler with homemade dumplings floating around in fresh fruit, I will quickly give up the pie and cookies for that fresh-made cobbler. You just can't beat blackberry or peach cobbler. Big, gorgeous cakes remind me of special celebrations, like Christmas, Easter, birthdays, and weddings. Cakes are appetizing with all the layers put together and tons of fluffy icing oozing out everywhere. I'm always tempted to take a slice. Heck, I'm getting hungry just writing this story!

Dessert and coffee gatherings are the easiest when it comes to entertaining. Mama would call neighbors and friends to come over for afternoon coffee and dessert. My Mama and Daddy liked to have coffee in the afternoons after their naps. Just the two of them together loving on each other over coffee. They continued this practice until they passed away (Mama at 85, and Daddy at 92).

Claude and Marcie Summerlin have given me a standing invitation to be at their home between 3 and 5 p.m. on any day. That's when they have their coffee. We sit on the front porch in rockers and just talk our lives away. It's not the fancy dessert or the great coffee that matters—it's all about friends and family gathering, just sharing stories and remembering old friends and family who once sat with you on that very same porch.

Don't worry about what size home you have or if it's kinda scattered. Folks don't care about that stuff. They want the fellowship, love, eye contact, and tight squeezes when they arrive. So, make that dessert, put on the coffee or tea, and call a loved one—call a friend or two—call that newcomer in your neighborhood. They will be tickled to be invited.

Sweets for the
Sweet
2022
B. Graff

TURTLE CHEESECAKE

———————

This is a perfect dessert for your Thanksgiving or Christmas table! You can use any kind of cookies you like for the crust—try chocolate graham crackers for a different flavor.

Crust:
1   sleeve graham crackers
20 gingersnaps
⅓   cup granulated sugar
6   tablespoons butter (salted or unsalted), softened

1. Preheat oven to 300°. Place a bowl of water in the oven when baking.
2. Place graham crackers and gingersnaps in a food processor and process until crushed into crumbs. You can also place them in a resealable plastic bag and crush them with a rolling pin.
3. In a bowl, combine the cookie crumbs, sugar, and softened butter. Mix until crumbs hold together.
4. Line the bottom of a 10-inch springform pan with parchment paper cut to fit. Press crumb mixture in bottom and up sides of pan.
5. Bake for 10 minutes. Let cool completely.

Filling:
5   (8-ounce) blocks cream cheese (room temperature)
1⅓ cups granulated sugar
1   tablespoon White Lily all-purpose flour
4   large eggs (room temperature)
1   teaspoon vanilla extract

1. In a large bowl, beat cream cheese, sugar, and flour with a mixer on low speed just until combined. Add eggs, one at a time, and vanilla, mixing just until blended. (Do not overmix—this will make your cheesecake crack!) Gently pour filling into baked crust.

Topping:
¼   cup packed brown sugar
¼   cup granulated sugar
⅓   cup chopped pecans, plus more for sprinkling on top
1   tablespoon White Lily all-purpose flour
2   tablespoons salted butter (melted)

Chocolate syrup
Caramel sauce (warm)

1. In a large bowl, stir together sugars, pecans, and flour. Add melted butter and stir until combined. Sprinkle topping over the top of filling.
2. Bake for 1 hour before checking. Cake is done when the center is set. Let cool completely.
3. When cheesecake is cool, drizzle with chocolate syrup and caramel sauce and sprinkle with pecans.

KITCHEN WISDOM

If you have never made a cheesecake, you may feel intimidated, but don't be! You can do this, and you will be all the better for your efforts! Even if it turns out ugly, it will taste good!

BANANA PUDDING

There are all kinds of banana pudding in the world today, but if you want the kind your granny made, this is it! The custard is unbelievable—I have to make myself extra so I don't eat it all before I put it in the dish!

1½ cups sugar
6 large eggs
1 tablespoon cornstarch
2 cups whole milk
1 teaspoon vanilla extract
3 bananas (sliced)
1 (11-ounce) box vanilla wafers (or less)

1. In a boiler, mix sugar, eggs, and cornstarch with a whisk. Slowly add milk, stirring well. Cook over medium heat, stirring with a spatula and scraping the bottom of pan constantly. The custard will begin to thicken. Continue to stir until the custard looks like thick buttermilk or pudding, about 8 to 10 minutes.
2. Remove it from the heat and add vanilla. Let the custard partly cool.
3. In a bowl or small casserole dish, put a layer of banana slices, a layer of vanilla wafers, and a layer of custard. Continue layering until all the custard is used. (You will probably have 3 layers.)

THE GRACE OF OUR LORD JESUS CHRIST BE WITH YOU ALL, AMEN.
—REVELATION 22:21, KJV

BREAD PUDDING

Bread pudding is always so good when you serve it right out of the oven. I've made it with white bread, leftover biscuits, and French bread—each way is delicious. My grandmother made bread pudding a lot when I was little. I didn't know it at the time, but I learned later that she liked to make it because she didn't want to waste any leftover or stale bread.

1 (16-ounce) loaf French bread, crust removed
5 large eggs
1 (15-ounce) can fruit cocktail (undrained)
¾ cup golden raisins
2½ cups sugar
4 cups whole milk
½ tablespoon ground cinnamon
Rum Sauce

1. Preheat oven to 350°.
2. Pinch bread into bite-size pieces (about 8 cups). (Don't squeeze it and make it hard. Loosely pinch it off so that it keeps its fluff.) Spread the bread pieces out in a 13x9-inch casserole dish greased with cooking spray.
3. In a separate bowl, crack your eggs and whisk them lightly. Then, add in the fruit, raisins, sugar, milk, and cinnamon and stir together.
4. Pour milk mixture over the bread and gently mix it all together. Make sure the bread is submerged in the milk mixture and let it set for 15 to 20 minutes.
5. Bake for 1 hour. Let it set for 15 minutes at room temperature. Serve with Rum Sauce poured over individual portions.

RUM SAUCE

2 sticks salted butter
1½ cups powdered sugar
1 teaspoon vanilla extract
2 tablespoons (or more) light or dark rum

1. In a small skillet, melt butter over low heat. Once melted, add powdered sugar and stir it well. Add in the vanilla and stir again. Lastly, stir in rum, 1 tablespoon at a time, until it reaches your desired taste.

William and Brenda celebrating a football game victory

FLAN

The first time I ate flan was at Dallas and Anna's home. It was beautiful and delicious. I love when recipes have fond memories that go along with them.

Caramel:
1 cup sugar
¼ cup water

1. In a saucepan, bring sugar and ¼ cup water to a boil. Stir constantly until liquid turns a brown color. Be careful not to burn the sugar. (When it's ready, the sugar mixture will become a hard ball when a little is dropped in cold water.)
2. Pour into bottom of heatproof round dish and set aside.

Custard:
8 egg yolks
2 egg whites
1 (14-ounce) can sweetened condensed milk
1 cup water
1 cup sugar
1 teaspoon vanilla extract

1. Preheat oven to 350°.
2. In a bowl, mix all ingredients together. Pour through a strainer on top of caramel in dish. Cover with foil. Place in a hot water bath.
3. Bake until firm, about 45 minutes. Let cool and invert flan onto a serving plate. (Make sure the serving plate is deep enough to hold caramel sauce.)

GRINCH CAKE

Working with what you have can apply to many different situations. My friend Mary Lynn Stone was excited to make a Red Velvet Cake for Christmas. After getting started, she realized she didn't have red food coloring! She looked in her cabinet and made a new plan— green food coloring for a Grinch Cake!

BE CAREFUL FOR NOTHING; BUT IN EVERYTHING BY PRAYER AND SUPPLICATION WITH THANKSGIVING LET YOUR REQUESTS BE MADE KNOWN UNTO GOD.
—PHILIPPIANS 4:6, KJV

LEMON CHEESE PIE

The great thing about this easy dessert is that you can top it with whatever you have. It's a no-cook, quick dessert! I like to serve this with lots of different toppings, like fresh fruit or chopped pecans and chocolate syrup.

1   (8-ounce) block cream cheese (room temperature)
1   (14-ounce) can sweetened condensed milk
⅓ cup fresh lemon juice
1   (6-ounce) package graham cracker piecrust

1. Mix cream cheese, condensed milk, and lemon juice. Pour into piecrust. Refrigerate for several hours until it firms.

THE PLATE

Most of you know my everyday plates are Fiestaware. They are bright and cheerful, and it's so much fun to collect all the colors. I can find them while I'm antiquing and going to yard sales.

I once heard a story that has stuck with me for a long time. Let me share it with you, for it has great meaning. An older couple had died and left all their belongings to their children. As the children were dividing all the items, they came to the plates, cups, and saucers of the fine china and the old cracked and worn-out everyday plates, cups, and saucers. None of the children or grandchildren wanted the fine china. They all wanted the old cracked and faded plates. Why? Because the cracked and broken plates brought back special memories of sitting around the kitchen table with their grandparents. Memories started flashing back, and tears started to fall from their eyes. They, themselves, remembered when the plate got the crack. They remembered setting the table with the old flowered plates. They remembered the great country dinners, the peas, fried okra, cornbread, and fresh sliced tomatoes that were on those old plates. Memories flowed that day!

As I think back about this story, I too have special memories of my childhood and the plates and glasses Mama and Grandmama used. Not paper, not plastic, but real glass plates that I still have today. What you use when you set your table matters! Memories are being made. Those memories can't be erased from the minds of those sitting at your table.

Leave this world and know in your heart that you did the best you could. As scripture says in Colossians 3:23, "And whatsoever ye do, do it heartily, as to the Lord." I think of this verse quite often. I will be doing something (putting on makeup, planting a flower, making my bed, hugging my loves, cooking in the kitchen, or setting the table) and think to myself, "Am I doing this to the best of my ability? Am I doing it unto the Lord?"

COCONUT CUSTARD PIE

This is a scrumptious pie that I used to like to make with my mama.
Isn't it so nice to have family recipes we can pass down through the generations?
The recipes don't have to be fancy—just good!

5 large eggs
1 cup sugar
1 tablespoon cornstarch
1 teaspoon vanilla extract
3 tablespoons salted butter (melted)
Pinch of salt
2 cups whole milk
1 cup sweetened flaked coconut
1 (9-inch) frozen piecrust or Homemade Piecrust (recipe on page 116)

1. Preheat oven to 350°.
2. In a bowl, beat eggs with a fork. Add sugar and cornstarch (see Kitchen Wisdom) and beat well. Add vanilla, melted butter, and pinch of salt and beat well. Add milk, a little at a time, while stirring. Add coconut and stir it in. Pour into piecrust but do not overfill.
3. Bake until pie has a slight jiggle in the middle, about 50 to 55 minutes. DO NOT OVERCOOK.

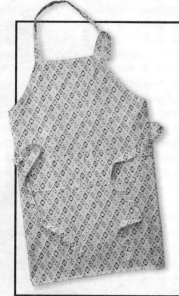

Apron Strings

I'm so thankful George and I shared our morning coffee together on the porch, sometimes wrapped up in a blanket to ward off the chill in the air. I'm thankful for the coffee and desserts I have had with Hannah in the afternoons. I'm thankful for each cup of coffee I've shared with Dallas on my front porch in the swing. I'm thankful for coffee with friends, young and old! And now, I'm older and enjoy my morning coffee with Jesus. It's our time to talk and my chance to listen to what He's saying to me. Time is fleeting, so spend time with friends and family loving, laughing, and enjoying great conversations. Build each other up in the Lord.

KITCHEN WISDOM

To dissolve the cornstarch, put it in a coffee cup with a little bit of whole milk. Use a fork to whisk it together. Keep adding milk, a little at a time, until the cornstarch is smooth and thin, then add it to the recipe.

HOMEMADE PIECRUST
You can do this, y'all!

Easy, quick, and cheap! With this recipe, you can make a pie any time you want without using a penny for gas money on a trip to the grocery store.

2½ cups White Lily all-purpose flour
1 cup salted butter (room temperature)
1 teaspoon sugar
5 tablespoons ice water

1. Preheat oven to 350°.
2. Mix flour, butter, and sugar together, stirring by hand. Add 5 tablespoons ice water and mix well.
3. On a floured work surface, knead the dough. Sprinkle a little extra flour around on the dough and surface if the dough seems sticky. Using a rolling pin, roll out the dough into a large circle with ⅛-inch thickness.
4. Place piecrust in a greased pie plate. Make sure that there are no air pockets between the crust and pie plate. (Flute pie if there is not a fluted dish. Prick the pie crust if you are baking it empty and adding filling later. If you are adding a filling to the uncooked pie crust, do not prick it.)
5. Bake until golden brown or follow the recipe for the pie you are making if there is filling in the pie.

— KITCHEN WISDOM —

Add more flour if your dough is sticky. If the dough cracks when putting it in your pie plate, just press it together with your fingers.

JAPANESE FRUIT PIE

Dallas and Hannah lived with my mother and daddy for a few months after they were grown. They had jobs near my parents. Mama would cook these Japanese Fruit Pies for them to go with black coffee. She enjoyed this special time she had with our children, and they enjoyed Papa and her.

1 stick salted butter (melted)
¾ cup sugar
2 large eggs (beaten)
1 teaspoon vanilla extract
½ cup sweetened flaked coconut
½ cup raisins
½ cup chopped pecans
1 unbaked piecrust

1. Preheat oven to 350°.
2. Mix together butter, sugar, eggs, vanilla, coconut, raisins, and pecans. Pour into unbaked piecrust.
3. Bake until golden and begins to set in the center, about 30 minutes.

50th wedding anniversary for Pickens and Evelyn Gantt

Wedding shower for Anna just before she became a Gantt

IF WE CONFESS OUR SINS, HE IS FAITHFUL AND JUST TO FORGIVE US OUR SINS, AND TO CLEANSE US FROM ALL UNRIGHTEOUSNESS.

—1 JOHN 1:9, KJV

SOPAIPILLA CHEESECAKE

—◆—

Cut this dessert in squares and serve it warm. Eat it slowly and enjoy the texture and flavor. It's good for your soul.

2   (8-ounce) cans refrigerated crescent dough sheet
2   (8-ounce) blocks cream cheese (room temperature)
⅔   cup plus ½ cup sugar, divided
1   teaspoon vanilla extract
¼   cup salted butter (melted)
2   teaspoons ground cinnamon

1. Preheat oven to 350°. Spray a 13x9-inch casserole dish with cooking spray.
2. Unroll 1 dough sheet and place in bottom of prepared dish (do not separate the rolls). Press seams of dough together and spread into the bottom and about ½ inch up all sides of dish.
3. In a bowl, beat cream cheese, ⅔ cup sugar, and vanilla with a mixer at medium speed until smooth. Spread cream cheese mixture on top of dough in dish.
4. Unroll remaining dough sheet onto a piece of parchment paper. Press seams together and spread until large enough to fit size of dish. Invert parchment and place dough sheet on top of cream cheese mixture in dish. Remove paper. Press top and bottom edges of dough sheets together, making sure seal is done on all sides.
5. Spread melted butter over the top of crust. Mix remaining ½ cup sugar and cinnamon together; sprinkle over melted butter. This will make the top crunchy.
6. Bake for 35 to 40 minutes.

Now faith is the substance of things hoped for, the evidence of things not seen.
—Hebrews 11:1, NKJV

Cape and Bay decorating a gingerbread house

WHITE CHOCOLATE SEET CAKE

One day, I was in the kitchen and decided to make up a new cake recipe. I'm so glad I did. It turned out wonderfully. Let your kitchen be your playground!

2¼ cups White Lily all-purpose flour
3¾ teaspoons baking powder
1 teaspoon salt
3 large eggs
1⅓ cups sugar
1 cup sour cream
1 (5.1-ounce) package cheesecake instant pudding mix
1 teaspoon vanilla extract
1 stick salted butter (melted)
½ cup whole milk
1 cup white chocolate chips
½ cup chopped praline pecans

1. Preheat oven to 350°. Grease a 13x9-inch casserole dish.
2. In a bowl, mix flour, baking powder, and salt. Set aside.
3. In a stand mixer, beat eggs, sugar, sour cream, pudding mix, vanilla, and butter at medium speed; mix well. Add in milk a little at a time. Add white chocolate chips and pecans. Lightly mix together.
4. Bake for 40 to 50 minutes.

Icing:
1 (8-ounce) block cream cheese (room temperature)
½ stick salted butter (room temperature)
1 teaspoon almond extract
2 cups powdered sugar
¼ cup chopped praline pecans

Garnish: white chocolate chips, chopped praline pecans

1. In a large bowl, mix cream cheese and butter. Add in almond extract and mix. Add powdered sugar a little at a time. Mix well. Spread icing on top of cake while the cake is still just a little warm. Garnish with chocolate chips and pecans on top.

chapter 5

RINGING IN THE NEW YEAR

PENNY IN THE PEAS

We all are gathered around the old farm table. Today starts a new year, a new beginning, and a fresh start. The old has passed, and a new year of adventures begins. It's Happy New Year at the Gantt family table.

Our thoughts are of things we need to do or not do this coming year. Lose weight, finish projects, improve relationships, get a new hairstyle, grow in our faith, or just be a better person—these thoughts are floating around in our minds. But, not today, we say. Today, we will celebrate and eat heavy, then rest afterward and rub our tummies.

As I'm cooking a big pot of black-eyed peas with hog jowl, I drop a shiny new penny in the pot. The old saying says that whoever finds the penny in their serving of peas will have good luck in the new year. I don't know where the tradition started, but I bet it was started to get the children to eat their black-eyed peas.

As the family had almost eaten their fill of the peas, no one had found the penny! George scooted back from the table, stood up, and headed straight to the kitchen. He then came back to the dinner table and sat back down. No one was paying any attention to George when he slid a penny into his serving of peas.

As he was scarfing down his peas he yelled, "Look, y'all! I found the penny!" All the children were so disappointed that they had not found the penny in their peas. About 10 seconds later, one of the grandchildren found the original penny in their peas. We all knew at that very moment that Big Daddy had tricked us all. That turkey had gone back to the kitchen to grab a penny and slid it into his serving of peas. He laughed at the kids! He had tricked them good. Laughter makes the best memories.

Our New Year's Day had started off with a BANG!

New Beginnings
2022
B. Grandt

BLACK-EYED PEAS
WITH HOG JOWL

—◆—

I'm 75 years old, and I have eaten black-eyed peas on New Year's Day all my life. I can't imagine not having them. I always cook my black-eyed peas with a piece of hog jowl floating in them for flavor, and I want cornbread swimming in the juice when I eat them—you can't get more Southern than this.

4   ounces hog jowl, left whole
2   quarts water
1   (16-ounce) bag dried black-eyed
    peas
Salt to taste

1. In a boiler, bring hog jowl and 2 quarts water to a boil; cook for 20 minutes to get the broth started.

2. In a colander, wash peas and then add them in with the hog jowl and broth.
3. Sprinkle in a small amount of salt. Cook over medium-low heat until the peas are nice and tender, about 2 hours and 30 minutes. You may have to add more water as the peas absorb lots of liquid.

Brenda ringing in the new year with Banks and Cape

Brenda and George—Happy New Year, Sweetheart!

MEMAMA'S CORNBREAD MUFFINS

Dallas loves MeMama's Cornbread Muffins split open with a piece of ham and a slice of onion in the middle. He says that it's his dessert.

Solid grease
1 cup White Lily self-rising cornmeal
1 cup White Lily self-rising flour
2 teaspoons sugar
1 teaspoon salt
3 teaspoons baking powder
2 large eggs (beaten)
1 cup whole buttermilk
¼ cup salted butter (melted)
Pepper Jelly

1. Preheat oven to 425°. Grease 1 (12-well) muffin pan with solid grease.

2. Mix cornmeal, flour, sugar, salt, baking powder, eggs, buttermilk, and butter together in a medium bowl.

3. Fill each prepared well two-thirds full with batter. Make sure that each well has about the same amount of batter so the muffins will all cook the same.

4. Bake until golden on top, about 12 to 15 minutes. Try to time taking the muffins out of the oven so you can serve them warm. Slather them up with butter and a dollop of Pepper Jelly.

PEPPER JELLY

Oh my, this stuff is so good with crunchy cornbread or served on top of cream cheese. Grow some peppers and make a batch. My son-in-law Walt loves pepper jelly!

¾ cup finely chopped bell peppers
¼ cup finely chopped hot peppers
1½ cups apple cider vinegar
5 cups sugar
1 (6-ounce) bottle fruit pectin
5 drops green liquid food coloring

1. Boil your ½-pint jars in hot water and then simmer them.

2. Put flats in a small saucepan. Bring to boil and then simmer. (Do not take the jars or the flats out of the water until the jelly is ready to go in the jar.)

3. In a medium saucepan, bring peppers, vinegar, and sugar to a rolling boil. Add pectin and boil for 5 minutes, stirring continuously. Add food coloring.

4. Put pepper mixture into prepared jars, filling one jar at a time. Place a hot flat on top of each jar and then screw on the rings. Place jars on a dish towel away from drafts.

TURNIP GREENS

—◆—

An old wives' tales says to eat lots of greens on New Year's Day, and you'll have lots of green money! I sometimes like to mix mustard greens with my turnip greens. Save the pot likker (the juices from cooked greens) when you're done and crumble some cornbread in it. You will not be disappointed!

2   big bundles fresh turnip greens (cut up) or 2 bags of precut turnip greens
2   quarts water
Salt to taste
5   slices fatback or streak of lean pork (wash each piece with water)

1. Thoroughly wash turnip greens.
2. In a large boiler, put in half of the turnip greens, 2 quarts water, salt, and pork. Cover with boiler lid and cook over medium heat. (You may not be able to get all the turnip greens in the pot at first, but flip turnips in pot a few times after they have been cooking a minute or two and they will wilt down.)
3. Add remaining turnip greens. Cook over medium-low heat until tender. (Make sure to have plenty of pot likker left to crumble your cornbread in.)

WHERE'D THEY GO?

George and I planted greens every year. One time, Gladys Davis, our preacher's wife, called and asked if she could pick her a mess of turnip greens. I said, "You sure can." I had not picked any yet. The next morning, after she had picked the day before, I decided to pick me a mess. Looking out the window at the patch, I noticed she had picked them all! I was so mad! I couldn't believe it! I went over to the garden, and what did I see? Deer tracks everywhere! It wasn't sweet Mrs. Gladys at all—it was a herd of hungry deer!

KITCHEN WISDOM

If you are blessed enough to find turnip roots, simply peel them, cut them into chunks, and let them cook or steam on top of the greens in the pot. They have a sweet flavor.

CARROT SALAD

I think we all love carrot salad—it's so good for us! And, this is a great dish to make if you need to carry a side to a church supper or to dinner at a friend's house.

5 large carrots (grated)
¾ cup raisins
1 Honeycrisp apple, unpeeled (diced) or 1 cup diced apple of your choice
1 cup mayonnaise
⅛ cup sugar

1. Mix all ingredients together and refrigerate. Stir just before serving.

IT IS WRITTEN, "MAN SHALL NOT LIVE BY BREAD ALONE, BUT BY EVERY WORD THAT PROCEEDETH OUT OF THE MOUTH OF GOD." —MATTHEW 4:4, KJV

KITCHEN WISDOM

Some apples have a thick peel. If you use those kinds, you will need to peel them. If I'm in a hurry, I like to grate the carrots in a food processor. It's quick and easy!

POOR MAN'S CAVIAR

Look at the ingredients! So, so good for you! It's called Poor Man's Caviar, but you'll feel mighty rich eating it. This is a good way to sneak in black-eyed peas on New Year's Day.

Marinade:
- ¾ cup balsamic vinegar
- ½ cup canola oil
- ¼ cup sugar
- 2 teaspoons salt
- 1 teaspoon black pepper

Caviar:
- 4 (15-ounce) cans black-eyed peas (drained and rinsed well)
- 1½ cups chopped tomato
- 1 cup chopped yellow bell pepper
- 1 cup chopped red bell pepper
- 1 (11-ounce) can white shoepeg corn (drained and rinsed well)
- 1 cup chopped red onion

Tortilla chips

1. For marinade: Combine all ingredients in a jar. Shake well to dissolve sugar.
2. For caviar: Place all ingredients in a bowl. Add marinade and toss. Cover and refrigerate for several hours. Serve with tortilla chips.

PEPPER SAUCE

There's nothing prettier than a jar of fresh Pepper Sauce sitting on the table. My family puts it on turnip greens and collards. If I forget to put it on the table, Hannah will always ask, "Mama, where's the pepper sauce?" And of course, I get up to find it!

Assorted whole hot peppers
    (enough to fill bottle)
Distilled white vinegar with 5% acidity
    (enough to fill bottle)
½   teaspoon sugar

1. Wash and dry peppers.
2. Fill a glass bottle completely with the peppers (putting small end of the pepper in first). Pack tight!
3. In a boiler, bring vinegar and sugar to a very hot temperature but not to a boil.
4. Immediately pour vinegar mixture over the peppers in the bottle. Seal the bottle with a cork or lid.
5. Let cool and store out on the counter at room temperature. Do not refrigerate.

KITCHEN WISDOM

When you're making your Pepper Sauce, sometimes, the vinegar will soak into the peppers quickly, so you may have to add a little more hot vinegar mixture 1 to 2 minutes after the initial pour. After you've used all your Pepper Sauce, if you can get the peppers out, put them in your cornbread! I hate to let anything go to waste.

FRIED PORK CHOPS

Pork chops are the perfect meat to go with your New Year's Day spread. I've even cooked boneless loin chops for breakfast with eggs, grits, and biscuits. Why not? They're so economical.

4   (½-inch-thick) bone-in pork chops (about 1 pound)
Salt and black pepper to taste
4   tablespoons whole buttermilk
1   cup While Lily all-purpose flour
½   cup vegetable oil

1. Place chops in a flat dish. Add salt and pepper to each side of each chop. Add 1 tablespoon buttermilk on top of each chop. Turn chops over and over until coated in buttermilk.

2. Coat each side of each chop in flour.
3. In a 12-inch cast-iron skillet, heat oil over medium-low heat. Gently add chops to the oil. Put a lid on the skillet. Cook until bottom side is medium brown, about 5 minutes. Using a thin spatula, carefully turn the chops to cook the other side. (If you turn the chop over with a fork or tongs, you may lose all the crust off the chop.) Remember, don't overcrowd the pan. You may need to cook in batches.

Apron Strings

When making resolutions, be sure to set attainable goals. For example, if you decide to lose weight, only set the goal for 5 or 10 pounds. Then, make a written plan of just how you intend to achieve this goal. Do you want to do without sweets? Or maybe cut portion sizes? With small changes, the goal can and will be achieved! Set your mind on being successful and intentional.

KITCHEN WISDOM

Many people overcook the chops, and this causes the chops to be dry and hard. Then, people think they don't like pork. Stop overcooking it, friends! You'll like it a lot better when it's cooked correctly.

FLO'S COBBLER

I love a cobbler that is juicy and delicious. This one is fit for a king and queen. Mama surely could make a fine cobbler. My daughter-in-law Anna has a sweet tooth, so she always likes this dessert, and I can't blame her! To make it even better, I like to serve it with a scoop of vanilla ice cream on top!

2 sticks salted butter
3 (14.25-ounce) cans fruit, undrained (about 4 cups)
2 cups White Lily self-rising flour
½ cup whole milk
5 tablespoons salted butter (melted)
1 cup sugar
2 cups water

1. Preheat oven to 350°.
2. Melt 2 sticks butter in a 3-quart casserole dish. Add fruit.
3. In a large bowl, mix together flour, milk, and 5 tablespoons melted butter with hands to make crust.
4. Roll out dough on a lightly floured surface to fit the size of your casserole dish. Place over the fruit mixture in dish.
5. In a bowl, mix sugar and 2 cups water. Pour sugar mixture over the crust.
6. Bake until bubbly and brown on top, about 30 to 40 minutes.

Anna and Dallas having snuggle time

Walt and Hannah as Masters of Ceremony at
The Red Garter Revue

SAUTÉED BRUSSELS SPROUTS

The brown sugar and lemon juice gives this dish a zesty "I want some more" taste. As George used to say, "this tastes more-ish!"

4   slices thick-cut bacon
1   pound Brussels sprouts
1   tablespoon minced garlic
½   lemon (juiced)
1   tablespoon brown sugar

1. Preheat oven to 400°.
2. In a 10-inch cast-iron skillet, cook bacon over medium heat until browned. Remove bacon and reserve 2 tablespoons drippings in the skillet.
3. Wash and trim Brussels sprouts. Cut in half lengthwise.
4. Heat bacon drippings over medium-high heat. Once hot, quickly add Brussels sprouts and garlic to the drippings and stir around. Sauté until Brussels sprouts begin to look charred, stirring frequently, about 4 minutes.
5. Bake for about 10 minutes. Crumble bacon. Put lemon juice, brown sugar, and bacon on top of sprouts and bake for 3 minutes more. Stir just before serving.

KNOW THIS, MY BELOVED
BROTHERS: LET EVERY PERSON
BE QUICK TO HEAR, SLOW TO
SPEAK, SLOW TO ANGER.
—JAMES 1:19, ESV

SNACK TIME

George said his grandmother kept baked sweet potatoes, a saucer of butter, and cornbread in the middle of her kitchen table at all times. She covered them up with a printed flour sack to keep the flies off. You could go pull back the sack and grab a snack any time you wanted to. I put my leftovers under a flour sack, too. My mama never did, so I don't know where I picked up the habit.

Brenda and George

BAKED SWEET POTATOES

I love making sweet potato patties and sweet potato casserole, but sometimes, you just want to bake a plain ole sweet potato. Some people eat them plain, and some people doctor them up with brown sugar, cinnamon, and butter. We love them with our New Year's Day meal.

6 or more sweet potatoes
Solid grease
Salted butter
Brown sugar
Ground cinnamon

1. Preheat oven to 400°.
2. Wash each potato and cover well with grease. Wrap each potato with foil and place in a big cast-iron skillet.
3. Bake until potatoes are tender, about 1 hour and 30 minutes, depending on how large the potatoes are. Stick a skewer in the potatoes after 1 hour to see if the potatoes are tender.
4. To serve, cut a slit down the length of each potato. Top with butter, brown sugar, and a dash of cinnamon, as desired.

AND NOW ABIDE FAITH, HOPE, LOVE, THESE THREE; BUT THE GREATEST OF THESE IS LOVE.
—1 CORINTHIANS 13:13, NKJV

chapter 6

WORK WITH WHAT YOU HAVE

CREATIVE COOKING

I've been preaching all my life to use what you have. When you do this, it saves time, money, and stress. Food is not wasted or thrown away when you use it all. It's a wonderful thing when you can create a casserole, soup, chowder, or dip from what you have in the refrigerator or pantry. Some of my very best dishes were made up recipes that I created in the spur of the moment. George would always say, "I hope you wrote this down! It's delicious!"

All the recipes in this chapter are made with just the staples. It's okay if you want to serve flapjacks and bacon for supper one night. Just relax, keep a stocked pantry, and cook with what you have on hand. You can do this, y'all!

George and Isabella

KITCHEN STAPLES

Sugar	Vinegar	Baking powder	Mayonnaise
Vanilla extract	Vegetable oil	All-purpose flour	Onions
Eggs	Solid grease	Self-rising flour	Cheese
Milk (sweet and buttermilk)	Self-rising cornmeal	Syrup	Powdered sugar
Bacon	Cocoa powder	Salt and pepper	Apples
Brown sugar	Butter	Raisins	Cinnamon
Garlic	Baking soda	Rice	Peanut butter
		Potatoes	Carrots

WHAT CAN I MAKE WITH JUST THE STAPLES?

Piecrust
Chocolate pie
Chocolate pudding
Chocolate cake
Buttermilk pie
Warm egg custard
Pancakes
Flapjacks
Rice pudding
Biscuits
Bread pudding
Hot water cornbread

Egg cornbread
Mayonnaise rolls
Creamed potatoes
French fries
Smothered fried
  potatoes
Roasted potatoes
Baked potatoes
Potato chowder
Hot chocolate
Sugar cookies

Scones
Hush puppies
White cake
Buttercream icing
Chocolate icing
Fried apple pies
Baked apples
Potato patties
Cheese biscuits
Fried dumplings
Stewed apples
Plate apple pie
Carrot apple salad
Eggnog
Peanut butter cookies
Apple cake
Apple coffee cake
Apple crisp
Lacy cornbread
Glazed carrots
Potato casserole
Quiche
Ants on a log
Fried rice

something
From Nothing 2022
B Gnatt

HOT WATER CORNBREAD

This cornbread is absolutely fabulous! You haven't lived until you've tried it! You can serve it with preserves, pepper jelly, or just plain.

8   tablespoons olive oil
1¼ cups White Lily self-rising cornmeal
¾   cup hot water

1. Preheat oven to 500°.
2. Pour 1 tablespoon oil in each section of a 9-inch wedge pan. Heat skillet over medium-high heat.
3. While the oil is getting very hot, mix cornmeal with ¾ cup hot water (use the hottest water that will come out of your kitchen faucet), stirring until the mixture is thin and watery.
4. When the oil in the skillet begins to smoke, take it off the heat and immediately put a serving spoonful of cornmeal mixture in each section.
5. Bake until cornbread is medium brown, about 10 to 12 minutes.

FOR BY ONE SPIRIT ARE WE ALL BAPTIZED INTO ONE BODY, WHETHER WE BE JEWS OR GENTILES, WHETHER WE BE BOND OR FREE; AND HAVE BEEN ALL MADE TO DRINK INTO ONE SPIRIT.

—1 CORINTHIANS 12:13, KJV

KITCHEN WISDOM

If you don't have a divided cast-iron skillet, you can use a regular cast-iron skillet and make just one big round of cornbread instead of wedges, like I do.

ME AND MY HAIR

My hair has been every color in the book, except green, every style, too. When I was a freckle-faced little girl, I had beautiful blonde hair. Mama always cut me some bangs. I guess that was a popular style for little girls in the 1940s and '50s. When the 1960s rolled around, home perms were a big hit. Glory, our house smelled like dead fish from the strong permanent wave solution. It floated through every room in our house.

Do y'all remember those tiny hard pink rollers that came with the home perms? Well, Mama had rolled my hair so tight with those things that my head stayed sore for days after. I remember sticking my head under the faucet in the kitchen sink to rinse out that awful smelling solution. What did I have after all this torture? A head full of tight curls!

As time passed, my hair became dishwater blonde, still full of kinky curls until I was at least the age of 12. Do y'all remember Lady Clairol? Well, during my years in Tuscaloosa County High School in Northport, Alabama, she was my friend! As a matter of fact, she was every girl's friend. Blonde was my color of choice. Mama did the color job at home, too!

The first time I ever went to a beauty shop was in 11th grade. Hating the style they gave me, I came straight home and washed out the 'do and never went back.

Life at Livingston State College gave way to a new color: platinum blonde. Back then, we all tried new hair colors. We even had wigs for bad hair days. Many times, we brushed out our hair on the top of an ironing board, covered the hair with a thin cloth, and ironed it to be straight. I was at Livingston State when I spied my George for the first time. I was hanging out the Webb Hall dorm window with other girls when I saw him. We had no screens on any of the windows, so we all hung out sitting on the windowsill of the third floor. He was wearing cutoff blue jean shorts, a flowered Hawaiian shirt, and buffalo sandals. Love at first sight. I had several classes with him. He asked me out for our first date.

I was getting tired of my platinum hair. So, off to the drugstore I went with several roommates. We picked the auburn brown dye off the rack of colors thinking it would look very near my natural color. We went back to the dorm and put the rinse on my hair. Oh no, it turned my hair turquoise blue! I washed and washed, but it wouldn't come out. In the '60s, we didn't have phones in our dorm rooms. I hurried down the stairs to the pay phone to call my mama. Hearing me cry my eyes out, she told me to come home. She took me to a color specialist. He informed me that he could not get it out but he'd cover it up. So, he dyed it black. It looked cheap to me, so I told him to cut my long hair off. He did! I ended up with a pixie style.

Now, I'm 75 and white-headed with still a small amount of auburn sprinkled in. The good thing about all my adventures with hair is that my George loved me through it all. He always told me, "Baby, I didn't marry you for your hair." It was true love!

FLAPJACKS

Mama used to make us Flapjacks for our breakfast. Now that I'm old, I look back and wonder if that's all she had to cook. Maybe we were poor, and I just didn't know it.

1   cup White Lily self-rising flour
1   large egg (beaten)
1½ cups whole buttermilk
1   tablespoon vegetable oil
Salted butter
Maple syrup
Fresh fruit

1. Mix flour, egg, and buttermilk.
2. In a cast-iron skillet, heat 1 tablespoon oil over medium heat. Drop a serving spoon size of the batter into the skillet. When brown on the bottom, turn over with a spatula.
3. Stack the flapjacks with 3 in each stack. Put a pat of butter and syrup on each stack. Serve with fresh fruit.

MAYONNAISE ROLLS

In any Southern home, mayonnaise is a staple! Use it in this recipe with just a couple of other ingredients for quick, easy, and tasty rolls!

1⅓ cups whole buttermilk
2 cups White Lily self-rising flour
⅓ cup mayonnaise
Salted butter (softened)

1. Preheat oven to 400°. Grease a 12-well muffin pan.
2. In a large bowl, combine buttermilk with flour. Stir in mayonnaise. Stir until moistened. Divide dough evenly into pan.
3. Bake until a light brown color, about 10 to 12 minutes. Serve warm with softened butter.

STUDENT TEACHING

When it was time to do my student teaching, Livingston State College sent me and some other girls to Linden, Alabama. We four girls rented a shotgun house to live in while we were there. This is where we invented Mayonnaise Rolls. At night, two of us would cook, and the other two would wash dishes. Without much money or time, we would stir up the ingredients and make rolls, then we'd slather them with butter when they came out of the oven and eat them warm! Eating these rolls now and remembering my time in Linden gives me such a good feeling inside.

SMOTHERED FRIED POTATOES

This is not a pretty dish, but talk about delicious! I can actually eat the entire skillet! It will want to stick on the bottom of the skillet, but that's okay. Continue to scrape it up and mix in with the rest of the potatoes—that's the "goodie," folks!

5 tablespoons oil (I like to use bacon grease for this dish)
5 large russet potatoes (cut into short, thick French fries)
1 large onion (cut into long slivers)
Salt and black pepper to taste
Ketchup

1. Pour oil into a 12-inch cast-iron skillet. Add potatoes to skillet. Place onions on top of the potatoes. Sprinkle with salt and pepper to taste. Put lid on the skillet (to smother the potatoes).
2. Cook over low heat until potatoes are tender, about 45 minutes. The potatoes will begin to break apart. Stir occasionally and then put lid back on skillet. The potatoes should be soft, not crunchy. Serve with ketchup.

Apron Strings

Live each day to the fullest. Open your eyes and see all the beautiful blessings God has put around you. Take that walk and see nature. Take that trip to see an old friend. Take time to see the sparkle in the eyes of the ones you love so dear.

KITCHEN WISDOM

We Southerners love to "smother fry" foods every now and then. What that means, whether you're talking about pork chops, chicken, or potatoes, is that you're frying something in a skillet with a lid on. The heat "smothers" it and keeps all the flavors in.

ROOT VEGETABLE BAKE

This is made from a little bit of this and a little bit of that, in terms of the root vegetable family. You can use whichever root vegetables you have on hand. Before you know it, you have enough to feed an army!

1 (1-pound) rutabaga (1-inch peeled cubed)
1 pound russet potatoes (1-inch peeled cubed)
1 pound turnip roots (1-inch peeled cubed)
1 pound carrots (1-inch peeled cubed)
1 large onion (cut into wedges)
3 tablespoons olive oil
½ tablespoon coarse kosher salt
¼ teaspoon black pepper
4 to 5 sprigs fresh rosemary (optional)
½ lemon

1. Preheat oven to 450°. Spray a rimmed baking sheet with a light coating of cooking spray.

2. Toss vegetables in olive oil, salt, pepper, and rosemary (if using). Pour vegetables onto prepared baking sheet.

3. Bake until vegetables are fork-tender and browned on the edges, 30 to 35 minutes, stirring every 10 to 15 minutes. Remove from oven and squeeze the lemon juice over the vegetables. Serve hot.

Hannah, Cape, Brenda, and Bay playing in the leaves

George straightening square nails

BAKED APPLES

The old saying goes, "an apple a day keeps the doctor away." One day when I came home from a long trip, the refrigerator was empty except for a few items. So, this is a dish I made up on that day—it hit the spot! It's so good!

3   Honeycrisp apples (unpeeled)
6   tablespoons brown sugar, divided
6   tablespoons salted butter, divided
Ground cinnamon
3   slices thick-cut bacon

1. Preheat oven to 350°.
2. Cut apples in halves. Scoop out a hole in the middle of each apple half, removing the core and seeds.
3. Place 1 tablespoon brown sugar in hole of each apple half. Put 1 tablespoon pat of butter on top of the brown sugar. Sprinkle a dash of cinnamon on each apple half. Cut bacon slices in half. Wrap 1 bacon slice half around each apple half.
4. Put the apple halves in a casserole dish small enough so that the apples will not lean to the side and lose all the goodies.
5. Bake until bacon is crisp and apple is very tender, about 40 minutes.
6. Serve each apple in a small bowl. Pour any juice left in the casserole dish over the apples.

WARM EGG CUSTARD

This is really an old-time recipe. Mamas of yesterday always had eggs, milk, sugar, and vanilla. So, this was something they could make at any time. This dessert feels good in your mouth.

8 large pasteurized eggs, separated (save egg whites to make Meringue)
2 cups sugar
4 cups whole milk
1½ teaspoons vanilla extract
Meringue

1. Mix egg yolks and sugar together in a boiler. Gradually add in milk, stirring with a whisk until all milk is in the boiler. Add vanilla.
2. Cook over medium-low heat, stirring often. Don't rush to cook the custard by increasing the heat. It will curdle if you do. Do not boil.

3. Pour warm custard in a pretty glass or cup and top with Meringue. Eat with a spoon.

MERINGUE

8 large pasteurized egg whites (from Warm Egg Custard)
¼ cup sugar

1. Beat egg whites with a mixer at high speed until stiff peaks form. Gradually add sugar, beating until well combined.

KITCHEN WISDOM

This meringue recipe has uncooked egg whites in it, so be sure to buy pasteurized eggs for this dish instead of using farm-fresh (which are great for other dishes!). Meringue makes desserts special.

BUNNY CHASING

When my Big Daddy, Cell Kirk Hicks, was a little boy he used what he had. He and other children his age had to find things to play with on hot summer days. Kick the can, hideouts, mule riding, rock throwing, and simple things like that entertained them.

On a warm spring day, a bunny rabbit ran across Cell Kirk's yard. He started to chase the bunny. Running as fast as he could, he probably was hoping to catch it and have it for a pet.

Big Daddy and Dallas

I surely wish I had asked my Big Daddy and Granny more questions before they both passed away—questions about life, beliefs, cooking, and all kinds of other things. Once our loved ones are gone, we can no longer ask them anything!

Anyway, Big Daddy was still chasing that rabbit when it suddenly ran into a stump hole. Little Cell Kirk rammed his hand into the stump hole to grab the bunny. A big, venomous snake was also in the hole. As his little hand went deeper into the hole, the snake bit two of his fingers. The doctor couldn't save the fingers, so little Cell Kirk lost Mr. Pointer and Mr. Tall Man.

He learned how to hold a pencil and a fork, and how to work with the fingers that were left. He adapted, grew up, married Miss Bertha Viola Jones, and raised three children.

I'm sure my Big Daddy got lots of stares as a boy. You know how children seem to stare at people who are different? Kids ask questions or are maybe are afraid to ask, but the staring will soon stop when we see the heart of the person. After a while, we don't even pay any attention to their abnormality.

In life, we all should look at the heart of folks. They have feelings, desires, and goals just like we do.

I guess my Granny Bertha looked past Big Daddy's hand that had missing fingers and saw the heart of the man she had grown to love. My Big Daddy worked with what he had, and we should, too!

BLESSED IS HE THAT READETH, AND THEY THAT HEAR THE WORDS OF THIS PROPHECY, AND KEEP THOSE THINGS WHICH ARE WRITTEN THEREIN: FOR THE TIME IS AT HAND.

—REVELATION 1:3, KJV

POTATO PATTIES

If you are lucky enough to have leftover creamed potatoes, you can use them in this recipe! These patties will be a hit with the whole family.

1½ cups creamed potatoes
1   large egg (beaten)
1   small onion (minced)
3   tablespoons White Lily self-rising flour
½   teaspoon salt
1   teaspoon black pepper
1   tablespoon oil

1. Mix potatoes, egg, onion, flour, salt, and pepper together.
2. Heat oil in a cast-iron skillet over medium heat. Add a 2-tablespoon scoop of potato mixture to the skillet. Fry until golden brown on bottom side. Turn patty over and fry on other side, pressing down slightly with a spatula. Once the patty is golden brown on both sides, it's ready to eat. Serve while hot!

FRENCH TOAST

Do you ever feel like you're in a rut? You may need to give yourself a jump start by spicing up your breakfast meal! Doesn't this look divine?

2	tablespoons salted butter
1	large egg (beaten)
⅓	cup whole milk
¼	teaspoon vanilla extract
1	tablespoon granulated sugar
Dash ground cinnamon	
3	slices white bread
Powdered sugar	
Maple syrup	
Fresh fruit	

1. In a cast-iron skillet, melt the butter over medium heat.

2. In a shallow dish, mix egg, milk, vanilla, granulated sugar, and cinnamon.

3. Dip each bread slice in the egg mixture, making sure each side is coated. Gently place the bread slices in the skillet side by side and cook over medium heat. Turn when bottom gets golden brown, and brown the other side.

4. Sprinkle powdered sugar on top and serve with syrup and fresh fruit.

RICE PUDDING

Waste not; want not! Use your leftover rice and surprise your family with this warm pudding. I promise they will love it!

3   large eggs
1   teaspoon vanilla extract
1   cup sugar
2   cups whole milk
½   stick unsalted butter (melted)
2   cups cooked rice
½   cup raisins

1. Preheat oven to 350°.
2. In a large bowl, mix together eggs, vanilla, and sugar. Add milk and melted butter. Add rice and raisins. Place mixture in a 2-quart baking dish.
3. Bake until slightly jiggly in the center, about 40 minutes. Do not overcook.

Grandbabies on a homemade waterslide

George swinging Isabella on a tree branch in the woods

Thus saith the LORD, let not the wise man glory in his wisdom, neither let the mighty man glory in his might, let not the rich man glory in his riches: But let him that glorieth glory in this, that he understandeth and knoweth me, that I am the LORD, which exercise loving kindness, judgment, and righteousness, in the earth: for in these things I delight, saith the LORD.
—Jeremiah 9:23–24, KJV

chapter 7

GOD'S BOUNTY

HE PROVIDES

The good Lord knew when He made us that we would desire a variety of foods. God sent manna (bread) from heaven to feed the Israelites, and they grumbled. So, God sent quail, and after a while, they grumbled again. Yes, He made us to love variety in foods and in life.

George and I were raised on good home-cooked meals of fresh meat and garden vegetables. We had deer, rabbit, squirrel, birds, and fish from off our land. So when Dallas and Hannah were born, they too were raised on the very same foods. It tickles me to see Hannah frying deer strips from a big deer that Walt has killed and cleaned for the freezer. I smile when Dallas and William have a big buck deer hanging on a rack ready to prepare meat for Anna to cook for their family. George taught Dallas and Walt how to skin and clean a deer. They, in turn, have taught their children. We are a family who believes in passing on the knowledge and skills that our parents taught us.

Brenda in the garden picking okra

Some folks live in big cities with tall buildings and no woods or land. They have to buy all their meat and vegetables at markets, and that's okay. Just keep buying and praising God at the markets for the meat, vegetables, fruits, and herbs that He has provided. I don't have a big garden anymore since George has passed away. But, I try to plant a few tomatoes, peppers, and squash—just to watch them grow and bloom, and to pick with my own two hands.

Thank you, Father, for providing for us all. Your bounty is amazing!

EVERYTHING THAT LIVES AND MOVES
ABOUT WILL BE FOOD FOR YOU. JUST AS
I GAVE YOU THE GREEN PLANTS, I NOW
GIVE YOU EVERYTHING.
—GENESIS 9:3, NIV

COUNTRY-FRIED DEER STRIPS

———

This is one of our family favorites. We're a family of hunters! We love eating venison (deer meat) because it's so healthy. The deer are grass-fed, and the meat doesn't have preservatives or any of that stuff. But, if you don't have venison, try country-frying beef—it will be great, too!

Vegetable oil
3   cups deer strips from the backstrap or tenderloin (about 4x½-inch-long pieces)
Salt and black pepper to taste
¼   cup whole buttermilk
1   cup White Lily flour (all-purpose or self-rising)

1. In an 8- or 10-inch cast-iron skillet, pour oil to a depth of ½ inch and heat over medium heat.
2. Place deer strips in a large bowl. Add salt, pepper, and buttermilk. Stir, making sure to coat every piece of meat. Add flour and flip, making sure all sides of the meat are coated well and not sticky. If sticky, simply add a skoot more flour and flip.
3. When oil is hot, gently add each piece of meat, shaking off excess flour back into the bowl. (Add a few at time to avoid overcrowding the skillet and making the temperature of the oil drop.)
4. Fry at medium heat until all sides are golden brown. Try not to stir much or it will tear the crunchy off the sides. Drain on paper towels.

A SOFT ANSWER TURNETH AWAY WRATH: BUT GRIEVOUS

WORDS STIR UP ANGER.

—PROVERBS 15:1, KJV

KITCHEN WISDOM

I cover my deer strips in water with 2 tablespoons salt before cooking. If you have time, let it soak overnight in the refrigerator. This process draws out most of the blood and the gamey taste. Drain the soaking water off and rinse well, squeezing excess water off before adding it to your work bowl.

KITCHEN WISDOM

Nothing goes better with Fried Catfish than Hush Puppies. You can find my recipe on page 144 of my first cookbook, *It's Gonna Be Good Y'all*.

FRIED CATFISH

Catfish are plentiful in Alabama. I remember sitting on the creek bank with my daddy waiting to catch a catfish to fry in the pan . . . I can taste it now. Daddy also made homemade fish traps to put in Coal Fire Creek in Pickens County, Alabama. He'd catch a big mess of fish of all kinds. At times, we have cooked catfish outside in a huge, black pot over a gas cooker. Any way you cook 'em, they're gonna be good!

6   fresh or frozen catfish fillets
Salt
1½   cups White Lily self-rising cornmeal
Vegetable oil
Ketchup

1. If catfish are frozen, thaw in a colander. Rinse catfish with water so the cornmeal has something to stick to. The catfish needs to come to room temperature so the temperature of the frying oil doesn't drop. Once thawed, salt each piece.
2. Put cornmeal in a large bowl. Place each fillet in the cornmeal, turning the catfish in the meal until each piece is coated well.
3. In a 4- or 5-inch deep cast-iron skillet, pour oil to three-fourths full. Heat oil over medium heat until it reaches 350° (or kind of rolling, if you don't have a thermometer). Take 1 fillet and shake it gently over the cornmeal bowl and then drop it gently into the hot oil. Fry until golden brown. (Most of the time, you can cook 3 fillets at a time.) Drain on paper towels. Serve with ketchup.

SMOTHERED FRIED QUAIL

———◆———

*This is a delicacy on cool nights. I love quail with grits, gravy, and biscuits.
When I was little, Daddy would go hunting with his bird dogs (Pete and
Kate) and bring home quail. Mama soaked them in salt water in the
refrigerator overnight, then she'd fry them for breakfast. The Lord provided.*

8   skinless quail (cleaned and washed)
Salt and black pepper to taste
¼   cup whole buttermilk
½   cup White Lily self-rising flour
Vegetable oil
Cooked grits
Quail Gravy

1. Separate the quail breast from the leg
section (the cook times are different).
2. Add salt and pepper to each piece and
place in a bowl. Add buttermilk and stir
to coat each piece. Add flour to quail and
coat well.
3. In a skillet, pour oil to a depth of
½ inch and heat over medium-low heat.
4. Place each quail breast (breast side up)
into the skillet. Place lid on skillet and
slowly fry, turning the breast when light
brown. Be careful not to knock off the
goodie when turning and don't overcook!
5. Fry the legs the same way. They don't
take as long since they are thinner.

QUAIL GRAVY

Vegetable oil from frying quail
2 to 3 tablespoons White Lily all-
    purpose flour
1½ to 3 cups water
Salt and pepper to taste

1. After frying quail, pour off some of
the oil, but leave ¼ inch to ½ inch in the
bottom of the skillet.
2. Add flour to oil in hot skillet. Cook on
medium heat, stirring constantly, until
golden brown. Whisk in water slowly,
stirring constantly, until thick and
bubbly. Continue stirring and add salt
and pepper to taste.
3. Let gravy continue cooking for just a
few minutes. Add more water, if needed.
When you've got the consistency you
like, it's ready to serve.

KITCHEN WISDOM

If you're using quail that someone has hunted and killed, remember to clean them really well. You
need to get out all the bird shot and feathers. You can also buy quail from many grocery stores. Even
if you don't have hunters in your life, try to find some quail and give this recipe a try!

RESTORING CAST IRON
You can do this, y'all!

Cooking in cast iron has become popular again, and I'm glad because it's the way people have cooked for generations! New cast iron can be expensive, so I suggest looking for cast iron at yard sales, antiques stores, and estate sales. A great thing about cast iron is that it can be restored and given a second life.

1. Start with your dirty cast-iron pot or pan. It's even okay if it has rust on it. This one came out of my barn, but it's got potential.

2. Put your pan down in some good soapy water—it needs to be really hot. Scrub with a stainless steel pad, but don't get the kind with copper in it because it tears up too easily.

3. Wash off any spiderwebs, dirt, and grime to start. Then, it's time to really scrub! It takes some elbow grease. Place a towel on the side of your sink to protect it while you scrub and to hold your pot in place.

4. Scrape it inside and out to get any layers of rust and grit off. Your water's going to get really dirty, but that's okay.

5. Once you get it clean, rinse it well. Double-check to make sure you got everything off. Dry it fully—that's important to keep it from rusting.

6. Take your newly cleaned skillet over to the stove. Turn your eye on high and put 2 pieces of bacon in your pan. The bacon will release oil that your skillet absorbs.

7. Use a fork to pull the bacon up around the sides. As the bacon heats and grease comes off, it will coat your cast iron. Be sure to coat the entire inside and outside with bacon grease.

8. Now, it's seasoned and ready to be used again! If this old skillet could talk, I wonder what it'd say. Who knows what's been cooked in it before!

FRIED GREEN BEANS

George and I planted bush green beans and running green beans. When I was in my 20s, the Covington County home extension lady came to our house and taught me how to can beans with my new pressure canner. What a joy—I canned enough for two years!

2   pounds fresh round green beans
¼   cup olive oil
2   tablespoons salted butter
Salt to taste
1   teaspoon garlic powder

1. Wash green beans and snip off end that was connected to the vine. Dry the beans with a cloth.

2. In a 10-inch cast-iron skillet, heat oil and butter on medium-low heat. Add beans and sprinkle with salt. Put a lid on the skillet and cook until beans are tender and crunchy, stirring often. When the beans are ready to eat, add garlic powder and stir; cook 2 to 3 minutes more.

STEWED APPLES

This dish has many uses. It can be served as a side with dinner, put over pancakes or biscuits as a topping, or used in fried pies! Apples are good for our health, so eat 'em up, folks!

8 large Pink Lady or Honeycrisp apples
½ cup water
½ cup sugar
Dash ground cinnamon
Butter

1. Peel the apples and cut into pieces.
2. In a boiler, cook apples with ½ cup water over low heat. Place lid on boiler. As apples cook and start to get tender, use the edge of a knife or a spatula to chop the apples up small. Continue cooking, but without a lid now, so that some of the moisture will cook out.
3. When the apples are good and tender, add sugar. Stir a time or two and then taste them. Add more sugar, a little at a time, until the apples taste good to you. After serving, some folks like a dash of cinnamon or a pat of butter on their apples.

PEAR PRESERVES

Mama and Daddy always looked forward to me coming to Tuscaloosa, Alabama, to visit and bringing them a couple of 5-gallon buckets of Kieffer pears from my trees. They would sharpen the kitchen knives to get ready to make preserves. You can't beat homemade preserves on a hot buttered biscuit.

8   cups Kieffer pears
6   cups sugar

1. Peel, core, and slice pears. Put them in a big boiler and cover with sugar. Cover with a cloth and let sit overnight on the kitchen counter.
2. The next morning, bring the pear mixture to a boil over medium-low heat, stirring gently to mix the juices from the pears and sugar. When the mixture comes to a boil, decrease the temperature to low and simmer until pears appear clear and pink and the syrup thickens, 3 to 4 hours.
3. While pears are cooking, go ahead and sterilize your pint jars and flats in boiling water.
4. When pears are ready, fill one jar at a time with the pear mixture. Wipe the rim of the jar with a clean, damp cloth after the pears are in the jar. Put the flat on the jar and then put on the ring. Set the jar on a cloth on the kitchen counter, away from any drafts. When you hear the lid pop, it means the jar has sealed. Continue this process until all jars are filled and sealed.

KITCHEN WISDOM

If one jar does not seal, just put it in the refrigerator and eat those preserves first. If you have pear syrup left in the pot, put it in a jar and have pear syrup on your pancakes.

STRAWBERRY GOO

This was one of my mama's recipes that I didn't make until recently. I love making recipes she made—it keeps our connection strong. This pie is fresh, light, and colorful. But, I'm warning y'all, it won't last long!

2¼ cups vanilla wafers (crushed)
1 cup powdered sugar
1 large egg
¼ cup salted butter (melted)
1 (5.1-ounce) box instant vanilla pudding mix
2½ cups whole milk
2 pints fresh strawberries, thinly sliced (about 4 cups)
1 cup heavy whipping cream
1 tablespoon granulated sugar

1. Preheat oven to 350°. Grease a 9x9-inch casserole dish.

2. Mix vanilla wafers, powdered sugar, egg, and melted butter to create a crust. Evenly press mixture into the bottom of the dish.

3. Bake until golden brown, about 10 to 15 minutes. Let cool.

4. Mix pudding as directed on box using 2½ cups milk. Pour into cooled crust. Top pudding with fresh strawberries.

5. Beat cream with a mixer at medium speed until peaks form. Add in 1 tablespoon granulated sugar and beat until stiff peaks form. Add cream mixture to top.

SNOW ICE CREAM

South Alabama rarely has any snow to speak of, but I know one thing for sure—when it snows, we all love snow ice cream. Mama would send us outside with a big metal bowl. We would gather the snow for Mama to mix up with milk, sugar, and vanilla. Oh my! How good it was! We'd sit by the fireplace and eat until our hearts' content.

Regular whole milk, condensed milk, evaporated milk, or eggnog leftover from Christmas
Sugar
Vanilla extract
8 to 12 cups fresh fallen snow

Banks, pretending it's Snow Ice Cream

1. In a small bowl, mix the milk of your choice with sugar and vanilla.
2. Take a large bowl outside and get fresh, very clean snow to bring back inside. Slowly pour the milk mixture over the snow while stirring. Eat immediately!

Note: The amount of sugar you'll need will depend on the type of milk you use. If you are using condensed milk or eggnog, you probably do not need to use any sugar at all.

LINE DANCING

My first line dancing class would soon be starting. I was feeling confident, believing I could succeed with lots of practice. If I can't, Banks can help me. She's amazing with any kind of dance. Probably that young brain helps a lot! Suddenly, I began to wonder if I could hold out for the two-hour class. Knowing that many of the other dancers had been in the class for years kinda put me in a tizzy. I knew they could hold out! Heck, there were tons of thoughts running through this head of mine. Determined to give it my best shot, I marched right through the door and into the class.

The Adult Activity Center provides a variety of activity choices, but line dancing was my first choice. Maybe it's because I've been dancing all my life—not in a fancy studio or having dance lessons as a child. My dancing started in our carport with all the other neighborhood children at Country Club Gables in Tuscaloosa, Alabama.

One Christmas, Santa brought me a little blue record player. It only played 45s, and I had collected a stack of Elvis records a foot high. We kids would dance on that concrete carport for hours. "Blue Suede Shoes," "Jailhouse Rock," "Hound Dog," "Heartbreak Hotel," and "Love Me Tender" could be heard by every Mama and Daddy all over the neighborhood. Yes, I was in love with Elvis—still am.

The yearly sock hop at our junior high was my next place to rock out. But, my very favorite place to dance was in our very own kitchen with my husband. I would be cooking

or at the sink washing dishes, and a slow groovy song would come on the radio. My George Gantt would ALWAYS grab me and hold me tight—dancing me all around the kitchen. Great memories. The one thing I learned from kitchen dancing is: Don't waste an opportunity—dance!

Guess I went off on a rabbit trail! Let's get back to line dancing. Making sure I stood in the back of the class so that no one's eyes would see my mistakes was where I thought I should be. But Mrs. Charlotte, our teacher, told me that new dancers needed to dance right slap kadab in the middle of the group. You see, in line dancing, we turn to a new wall all through the dance. So, if I were in the middle, I would always have an experienced dancer around me. You know—the one who already knows the ropes!

Now, I have three years of line dancing under my belt! Mrs. Charlotte is always challenging us with a brand-new dance. She says it's to keep our brain muscles working. Can't argue with that! The ladies are uplifting and encouraging, always giggling, smiling, and having a great time. We also have amazing conversations during our water breaks. We all laugh when Mrs. Charlotte says if you don't know the next step, just stand there and wiggle until you see a move you remember. Y'all know I have to stand in the middle quite often and wiggle while the others dance around me. God gave us rhythm! Some play instruments, some sing, some clap, and some dance. So, stomp that foot, you'll feel much better knowing you tried.

MEMAMA'S SQUASH PICKLES

These pickles need to be refrigerated overnight before serving. Get you a plateful of purple hull peas with a side of MeMama's Squash Pickles, and you'll have yourself a winner!

6   cups yellow squash (sliced into very thin circles)
6   cups zucchini (sliced into very thin circles)
2   onions (cut into slivers)
1   bell pepper (cut into thin slivers)
1   tablespoon pickling salt
3   cups white vinegar
4½ cups sugar
2   teaspoons celery seed
2   teaspoons mustard seed

1. In a large bowl, combine squash, zucchini, onions, and bell pepper. Cover with water and add pickling salt. Let stand for 1 hour. Drain vegetables very well, using a colander. Return vegetables to large bowl.

2. In a large boiler, bring vinegar, sugar, celery seed, and mustard seed to a rolling boil over medium-high heat. Remove from the heat. Add the vinegar mixture to the vegetables and let stand for 2 hours.

3. Go ahead and sterilize your pint jars and flats in boiling water.

4. Using a slotted spoon, put the vegetables into the pint jars, one pint at a time, filling jars to within ¼ inch of the top.

5. Pour vinegar mixture to boiler. Bring vinegar mixture back to a boil over medium-high heat. Ladle vinegar mixture over vegetables in the jars, leaving ¼-inch space. Wipe jar rims with a clean cloth. Place the flats on the jar. Then, put on the rings. Continue until all jars are filled.

6. Then, cook jars for 20 minutes in a water bath. Remove jars from water bath and place on a kitchen towel, away from any drafts.

WATER BATHS

Water baths are important for canning. You need to fill a very large pot with enough water to cover three-fourths the height of your jar. Place a round rack on a thick folded hand towel in the water on the bottom of the boiler. Heat the water to a good simmer temperature. On your countertop, fill jars (they need to be hot already) with hot food, then add the lids and rings to the jars. Immediately place each jar into the boiler of simmering water. Continue until the boiler is full of jars, but do not let the jars touch one another. The water should be at least 1 inch over the tops of your jars after all the jars are added. If not, add more hot water to the pot.

Turn the heat up to a boil—let boil for 20 minutes then turn the heat off and let the jars just sit in the hot water for 10 to 20 minutes. Then, carefully take the jars out of the water and sit them on your counter on a towel, out of any drafts. Do not disturb the jars for 12 to 24 hours. Then, press down on each lid. If it's already down or stays down when you press it, that means it sealed. If it didn't seal, place that jar in the refrigerator and eat it within 2 weeks.

Only foods with high acidity, like some fruits and vegetables, need water baths. All other foods need pressure canning.

FRESH BLUEBERRY PIE

I recently bought eight blueberry bushes and planted them at The Cottle House Bed & Breakfast so I could have fresh berries of my own! We are never too old to plant trees, bushes, and flowers for the next generation to enjoy.

3 cups fresh blueberries
1 cup White Lily all-purpose flour (for coating berries)
Homemade Piecrust (recipe on page 116)
¾ cup sugar, plus more for sprinkling
1 stick salted butter, divided
Vanilla ice cream

1. Preheat oven to 350°.
2. Rinse off blueberries and let drain. Once drained, place berries in a bowl and toss with flour coating each berry completely. (The berries need to be damp so the flour will stick.)
3. Using a rolling pin, roll out the dough into a large circle with ⅛-inch thickness. Place dough in pie plate, trimming the excess edges. Gather trimmings and roll to a 10-inch circle. Cut the dough into 10 strips for the lattice crust on top.
4. Put the coated berries in the pie shell, shaking off excess flour back into the bowl.
5. Evenly sprinkle sugar on top of the berries. Cut ½ stick butter into small pats and put on top of the sugar.
6. Put dough strips on top of the pie and do lattice work by layering them and crimping the edges. Smear remaining ½ stick butter over the crust and sprinkle just a little sugar on the crust.
7. Bake until crust is golden brown. Top with ice cream.

Apron Strings

God is so good and blesses us with the things we need. But, be careful not to let your home become overcrowded with "stuff." Your home should be a relaxing, peaceful sanctuary with NO clutter. Clutter causes stress and can cause you to lose things you need. Clutter can make you feel like saying, "I don't know where to start cleaning." Here is my advice: don't buy things you don't need, and give away things you're not using. Don't clean your house until you've gotten rid of all the clutter. Now, get started!

KITCHEN WISDOM

When summertime comes and you need a recipe for your Fourth of July picnic, there's nothing better than a beautiful Fresh Blueberry Pie! There may be a blueberry farm nearby—pick your own!

chapter 8

FRONT PORCH SITTING

BRING BACK THE FRONT PORCH

I read an article one time that asked a question: "What happened to the front porches in America?" It got me to thinking! I started remembering times when we had front porches. When friends would pass by and see us on our porch, they'd stop and visit a while, have a glass of tea, and just talk. The time was wonderful for bonding and relaxing, laughing, and telling stories. It was good for children and teens, too. Even they would sit among the adults and listen to our conversations and sometimes join in.

Things are different today! Many people have gotten rid of their front porches and built large decks on the backs of their houses. Now, folks won't stop because they feel like they might be intruding. Many teens today have not developed the art of conversation. They may literally sit in the same room with their friends and text the friend sitting across the room from them—how awful is that! I've seen husbands and wives on dates at restaurants, both staring at their phones and not looking up, either! When George and I went on dates, we always sat across from each other so that we could talk while looking into each other's eyes. God made us for companionship.

Bring back the front porch is what I say! Sit in the rockers, swing on the porch swing, churn the ice cream, and eat the snack. Invite folks to sit a spell, shell the peas, rock the babies, or take a nap. There are so many options, so do whatever you want to do! It's time to bring back the front porch!

Bay, Isabella, and Cape

THE CHRISTIAN FAMILY

WIVES, SUBMIT YOURSELVES UNTO YOUR OWN HUSBANDS, AS IT IS FIT IN THE LORD.

HUSBANDS, LOVE YOUR WIVES, AND BE NOT BITTER AGAINST THEM.

CHILDREN, OBEY YOUR PARENTS IN ALL THINGS: FOR THIS IS WELL PLEASING UNTO THE LORD.

FATHERS, PROVOKE NOT YOUR CHILDREN TO ANGER, LEST THEY BE DISCOURAGED.

—COLOSSIANS 3:18–21, KJV

REFRIGERATOR PECAN COOKIES

You can make this dough up ahead of time and then bake the cookies at the last minute if company shows up. They're great for front porch sitting!

5   cups White Lily all-purpose flour
1   teaspoon baking powder
1   tablespoon baking soda
2   cups salted butter (softened)
2   cups brown sugar
2   cups granulated sugar
2   large eggs
1   tablespoon vanilla extract
2   cups chopped pecans

1. Mix flour, baking powder, and baking soda together.
2. Mix butter, brown sugar, granulated sugar, eggs, and vanilla together.
3. Add flour mixture, a little at a time, to sugar mixture. Add pecans. Roll dough into logs and refrigerate for at least 1 hour.
4. Preheat oven to 325°.
5. Cut logs into ¼-inch-thick slices and place 1 inch apart on greased baking sheets. Bake for 8 to 10 minutes.

NOW UNTO HIM THAT IS ABLE TO KEEP YOU FROM FALLING, AND TO PRESENT YOU FAULTLESS BEFORE THE PRESENCE OF HIS GLORY WITH EXCEEDING JOY, TO THE ONLY WISE GOD OUR SAVIOUR, BE GLORY AND MAJESTY, DOMINION AND POWER, BOTH NOW AND EVER. AMEN.
—JUDE 1:24–25, KJV

CANDY BAR ICE CREAM

Everybody loves ice cream! And, everybody loves candy! Marry them together, and what do you get? This delicious ice cream to enjoy on the porch!

6   large eggs
2   cups sugar
1   (14-ounce) can sweetened condensed milk
½   cup creamy peanut butter
½   pint heavy whipping cream
6   cups whole milk
6   (1.9-ounce) chocolate-covered peanut butter wafer candy bars (crushed)

1. Beat eggs with a mixer at medium speed. Add sugar and beat until smooth. Pour in sweetened condensed milk and stir until smooth. Add peanut butter and cream.

2. Pour mixture into the can of an ice cream maker and fill with milk. Add crushed candy bars in last and stir. Freeze as usual according to your machine's instructions.

Cape, George, William, Isabella, Dallas, Banks, and Bay

Cape, Brenda, Hannah, and Bay

KITCHEN WISDOM

I use Butterfinger® candy bars for this ice cream. I always put my candy bars in a gallon-size resealable plastic bag and beat it with a rolling pin to crush the candy into small to fine pieces. It keeps the mess from going everywhere!

He had always been good and kind to all the other monsters in the Deep Dark Scary woods.

The little green monster wanted to meet some children to play with. Scaring children was certainly not what he ever wanted to do. He only wanted to play with them and to be a friendly little monster.

3

ARTISTIC LIVING

People say, "variety is the spice of life." Maybe that explains my desire to paint the unusual—oyster shells, seashells, door panels, metal, old wood, paint buckets—you can paint on anything! As the old saying goes, "an idle mind is the devil's workshop." Keep those hands busy making whatever your heart desires—then give it away. You'll be happy, and so will the receiver. Remember to always sign and date your work.

– Page 7   The Democrat-Reporter

View from the hill

She creates real work of art on eggs

Linden,

Egg decorating is not a new art. In museums around the world, there are collections of jeweled decorated eggs owned by queens and beautiful ladies of past centuries.

Until a decade ago, egg decorating in America was the craft of only a few, but it is now widely-spread. Many craft magazines have "kits" which may be ordered and put together by those who do not have the desire or talent for design.

Brenda Gantt, who lives with her husband and two small children in Green Meadows, does have a talent and that designed and painted eggs that are a real work of art.

This personable young mother and wife took art at Livingston University, but says her oil paintings look like "child's work."

She may not be able to create an oil painting that is pleasing, but the dainty and delicate eggs she has decorated and painted are pleasing and beautiful to the eye.

She "blew" the eggs, which to some of us who have tried, is an art itself. The egg is emptied of the yolk and white by carefully punching holes in both ends of the egg with a

needle and blowing the egg into a cup. Then the empty shell is washed and ready to be decorated.

Brenda painted flowers on the eggs she has, and the acrylic paints she uses adds a raised effect to the eggshell. Iris, daisies, and tulips, are some of the flowers she paints. Narrow velveteen ribbon covers the tiny holes and makes

loops to hang the eggs.

Brenda has presented relatives with some of the eggs she has painted, but has one "tree" for her family to enjoy. The "trees" are inexpensive mug holders.

All through Brenda's house are touches of original decorating ideas and some special crafts. She and her husband George, decorated

tures from 45 year old newspapers that are interesting examples of what decoupage should really look like.

When their two pre-schoolers are older, Brenda plans to teach and is well-pr...
she holds.

Brenda Gantt of Linden artistically paints eggshells into creative decorations for her home and for gifts. Her daughter, Hannah, is pictured with her.

This Business of Birthdays
All Started With Adam.

And Since He Began It
We've All Had 'em.

But Even Though Some Folks
Let Birthdays Upset 'em.

The Best Thing To Do
Is Take And Enjoy 'em.

Cecil's Turning 90!
Flo's Turning 84!
So, Be On Time And
Arrive At Our Door.

We'll Have Lunch Cooked
We'll Eat Together
We'll Have Fun
Know Matter The Weather.

September 18, 2010
2516 Shole Place
11:30 A.M.
Your Presence Is Present Enough

Celebrate
With
Cecil & Flo

RSVP - Flo Hicks 339-2247

To Benns
Love
"Big Mama 4"
Brenda Ann Hicks Gantt

GARBAGE DIP

This dip has everything but the kitchen sink in it! Get a big spoonful and plop it on a corn chip.
I guarantee, you will go back for more!

6 tomatoes (chopped)
1 bell pepper (chopped)
1 Vidalia onion (chopped)
1 (16-ounce) bag carrots (peeled and grated)
1 (4.5-ounce) can chopped green chiles
Salt and black pepper to taste
Garlic powder to taste

1 (8-ounce) bottle Italian dressing
Corn chips

1. Mix tomatoes, bell pepper, onion, carrot, green chiles together. Add salt, black pepper, and garlic powder to taste. Pour in Italian dressing and stir. Serve with your favorite corn chips.

HANNAH'S CHUNKY GUACAMOLE

One afternoon, Hannah had made this recipe and called for me to come over. We realized we didn't have any chips to eat it with! So, I made Lacy Cornbread (in my first book, It's Gonna Be Good Y'all, on page 48) to eat it with—it was a perfect combination for back porch munching!

4　ripe avocados
½　cup finely chopped tomato
½　cup finely chopped fresh cilantro
½　lemon (juiced)
¾　teaspoon garlic salt
Tortilla chips

1. Cut avocados in half lengthwise and remove pit. With a spoon, remove avocado flesh and place in a bowl. With the tines of a fork, mash avocado until chunky.
2. Add tomato, cilantro, lemon juice, and garlic salt, and stir. Serve with tortilla chips or heap it up on your favorite tacos.

STUFFED MUSHROOMS

I wasn't raised on Stuffed Mushrooms. George and I didn't serve them to our children either. But, within the last 20 years, I have grown to love them. I can't remember where or when I was introduced to them, but thank goodness I found out about them from somewhere—I could eat a platterful! They're great porch finger foods.

2 (8-ounce) packages fresh whole baby bella or white mushrooms
8 ounces or ½ roll pork sausage
1 (8-ounce) block cream cheese, softened
1 cup packed fresh spinach leaves (finely chopped)
1½ tablespoons Worcestershire sauce
⅛ teaspoon garlic salt

1. Preheat oven to 350°.
2. Wash mushrooms and carefully remove stems from caps. Save about 12 stems and finely chop them.

3. Fry and drain the pork sausage.
4. Combine cream cheese, sausage, chopped mushroom stems, spinach, Worcestershire, and garlic salt. Put a spoonful of the sausage mixture into each mushroom cap and place mushrooms in a casserole dish.
5. Bake for 20 to 25 minutes.

Brenda, Bay, Banks, Isabella, and Cape

BIRDS ALL DAY AND CRICKETS AT NIGHT

When we first built our house in 1975, we were in our early twenties. We didn't know one thing about house-building, so we wound up with a tiny front porch! It hardly had room for a rocker. I hated not being able to enjoy it. It was just too small. About 20 years passed, and then Hurricane Opal hit us really hard here in Andalusia, Alabama. She knocked off our front porch, and we had other terrible damage. George said, "Okay, Baby, you've always wanted a big front porch. I'll build it back big, if you like. If not, I never want to hear another word about that tiny porch." Now, I have a wonderful, big porch—it's got a dining table, three rockers, and a swing! I've got plants, decorations, and small tables for sipping our afternoon sweet tea or morning coffee on. We see and hear birds in the day and crickets at night. God took ashes and made beauty. I get to enjoy so much of it from my front porch.

WATERMELON BASKET

This is a cool, healthy summertime treat. It's also something you can do with your children. They will feel so proud of the way it turns out. Isabella loves all fruit, so naturally, this is her favorite.

1   long watermelon
2   cups cubed fresh pineapple
2   cups sliced fresh strawberries
2   cups fresh blueberries
2   cups green grapes
2   cups purple grapes
2   cups chopped cantaloupe
2   cups chopped honeydew melon

1. Using a sharp knife, cut a thin slice from the bottom of the watermelon, so it sits flat. Mark a horizontal cutting line 2 inches above the center lengthwise around the watermelon.

2. To make the basket handle, using a sharp knife, score a 1½-inch-wide strip widthwise across the top of melon, connecting both sides to the horizontal line.

3. With a long, sharp knife, cut all the way through the rind above the cutting lines in a zigzag pattern. Carefully lift off the side pieces. Remove fruit from both sections and cut into balls. Refrigerate the watermelon basket.

4. To arrange, fill the basket with remaining ingredients and watermelon balls just before serving.

NEW FAME People say to me, "You're famous!" I guess in the eyes of many that is the case, but in my eyes and the eyes of family and friends, I am just Brenda, Mrs. Gantt, Mama, Big Mama, and Aunt Brenda. I know that I'm just a regular lady trying to do the Lord's will. I've always known that the Lord opens doors for us to walk through. He alone opened this Cooking with Brenda Gantt Facebook show. It certainly wasn't something I dreamed up.

Focusing on helping men, women, and children to be successful in their kitchens is one of my goals. But, I believe the Lord has a plan to help others know about His great love for them through the show. Many of you have memorized John 3:16, "For God so loved the world, that He gave his only begotten Son, that whosoever believeth in Him should not perish, but have everlasting life."

This verse humbles me, for I know that we all have purpose. We all are loved. We all have a door to walk through. We all are equal in the eyes of the Lord. So, I ask myself, "Am I famous like people say?" My answer is, "No." I'm just a Southern cook that many folks know. They've watched the cooking show, and through the show, we have connected to each other. I hear their hearts through comments on Facebook, and they hear mine. I'm thankful for the opportunity to be part of others' lives through this unexpected open door.

STRAWBERRY SHORTCAKE

To me, this is strictly a warm-weather treat. In the spring and summer, the strawberries are red all the way through! We're lucky to have strawberry farms in Alabama so that we can get fresh red strawberries each year.

2 pints fresh strawberries (sliced)
¼ cup sugar
Pound Cake
Vanilla ice cream
Whipped topping

1. In a large bowl, mix strawberries and sugar. Refrigerate for 15 minutes and then stir again.
2. For each serving, slice the pound cake and place one slice on a plate. Top with strawberry mixture. Top with 1 scoop ice cream. Top with whipped topping and 1 strawberry slice.

Apron Strings

As I've gotten older, I've learned that it's really important to be yourself. You are special—one of a kind! There is no one like you. Get up in the morning with an attitude of thankfulness in your heart. Whatever you do today, give it your very best!

JESUS SAITH UNTO HIM, THOMAS, BECAUSE THOU HAST SEEN ME, THOU HAST BELIEVED: BLESSED ARE THEY THAT HAVE NOT SEEN, AND YET HAVE BELIEVED.
—JOHN 20:29, KJV

KITCHEN WISDOM

I always make a homemade pound cake to use for this recipe. My favorite is Flo's Pound Cake. You can find this recipe on page 37 of my first book, *It's Gonna Be Good Y'all*. But, any store-bought or boxed cake mix will work for Strawberry Shortcake!

PEANUT BUTTER COOKIES

The cafeteria in our elementary school always made Peanut Butter Cookies once a week. Honey, you could smell 'em baking all in the hallways and in every classroom. I was one excited little girl when lunchtime arrived.

½ cup salted butter, softened
½ cup creamy peanut butter
½ cup granulated sugar, plus more for rolling
½ cup brown sugar
1 large egg
½ teaspoon vanilla extract
1¼ cups White Lily all-purpose flour (sifted)
¾ teaspoon baking soda
¼ teaspoon salt

1. Preheat oven to 375°.
2. Beat butter, peanut butter, sugars, egg, and vanilla with a mixer at medium speed.
3. Sift together flour, baking soda, and salt. Add flour mixture to peanut butter mixture, beating until blended.
4. Shape batter into 1-inch balls. Roll each ball in granulated sugar. Place 2 inches apart on an ungreased baking sheet. Press each ball with fork tines (dip fork in flour first) in a crisscross design.
5. Bake for 10 to 12 minutes. Let cool.

George and his baby brother, Kyle

KITCHEN WISDOM

When I got home from school and we didn't have a lot of snacks around, Mama would say, "Go fix yourself a peanut butter spoon." That meant to stick your spoon down in the peanut butter and pull out a big gob of it, then go outside and eat it slowly like it's a special treat—and it was! Next time your kids or grandkids need a snack, give it a try!

BOILED PEANUTS

The South is known for peanut boils. We all look forward to our farmers taking their tractors and plowing up their peanuts—that means a peanut boil is coming soon! They're perfect for football tailgate parties in the fall, and of course, our front porches.

3   pounds dry peanuts in the hull
½   cup plus 1 tablespoon salt

1. In a 22-quart boiler pot, bring peanuts, salt, and water to cover to a hard boil. Decrease heat to medium and cook, stirring occasionally. At first, the peanuts will try to float, so push them down with a spoon into the salty water. Additional water may need to be added to the boiler after 1 hour of cooking. You will have to continue adding water as it will cook away.
2. After about 6 hours, get 1 peanut out of the boiler and open it up. Eat it; if it's not very tender, continue to let the peanuts boil until tender.

A GOOD MAN LEAVETH AN
INHERITANCE TO HIS CHILDREN'S
CHILDREN: AND THE WEALTH OF THE
SINNER IS LAID UP FOR THE JUST.
—PROVERBS 13:22, KJV

KITCHEN WISDOM

This recipe takes a long time. If you're not going to be home for a good part of the day, you can try cooking them in a slow cooker—then they'll be ready when you walk in the door! Also, there is a big difference in boiling time of green peanuts (just dug up) and dry peanuts (been dug up and dried).

~∾⦿∾~

chapter 9

PICNIC

SWEET SUMMER MEMORIES

It doesn't have to be a feast or a big event. Just a pack of crackers, water, a quilt, and a place, and voilà—you have a picnic!

I remember when Dallas and Hannah were little, we had a picnic almost every day. Being a teacher, I didn't work during the summertime, so we would grab a basket, fill it with sandwich makings, drinks, fruit, chips, pickles, and whatever else we had in the pantry and head out to "Point A." There were picnic tables and a lake we could swim in. The three of us had the best time.

You see, George was at work, so we would go picnicking in the morning time, but we'd make sure we were back home in time to cook a good family supper. Years later, when the grandchildren came to our home, we had many picnics! George and I would take them to Point A, or we'd just pack a basket and head to the woods behind our house. There is nothing quite like lying on a quilt in a Southern pine thicket when you've got a nice breeze, the smell of pine straw, the blue sky above, and pine branches moving in the wind.

Brenda and George with the grandbabies

The children loved it . . . minus the red bugs. During the summer, we would paint the bugbites on our skin with red nail polish. We had dots all over us. I miss those unplanned picnics in the woods.

George and I had picnics together, too. No children, just the two of us. God never said marriage would be easy. Marriage needs to be cultivated, worked at, and appreciated. I can't think of a better way to enhance a marriage than a good old-fashioned picnic. So, pack the food, head to the woods with your love, and spread that quilt.

WHILE WE LOOK NOT AT THE THINGS WHICH ARE SEEN, BUT AT THE THINGS
WHICH ARE NOT SEEN: FOR THE THINGS WHICH ARE SEEN ARE TEMPORAL;
BUT THE THINGS WHICH ARE NOT SEEN ARE ETERNAL.
—2 CORINTHIANS 4:18, KJV

HAM SPREAD

This is such an easy thing to make and take on picnics. You can eat it with crackers or even put it on a sandwich. I always make this after I cook a big ham for Sunday dinner. Use those leftovers!

4 cups ham (finely chopped in a food processor)
1 cup mayonnaise
1 cup sweet pickle relish (drained)
Round buttery crackers

1. Mix chopped ham and mayonnaise together in a bowl. Add pickle relish and stir well.
2. To serve, top a round buttery cracker with the spread and enjoy!

Walt, Hannah, Banks, and Dallas

Fourth of July Parade in Andalusia, Alabama

KITCHEN WISDOM

There are many things you can add to the spread in addition to sweet pickle relish. Try diced onion, olives, or chopped jalapeños. Get creative and add in whatever sounds good to you and your family!

PIMENTO CHEESE

I have to fix me five or six Pimento Cheese crackers, put them on a saucer and then put the Pimento Cheese back in the refrigerator. Why, you ask? Because I will eat about a half a sleeve of crackers and Pimento Cheese if I don't get it out of my sight! I love that stuff.

1 (16-ounce) block extra-sharp Cheddar cheese
1 (8-ounce) block mild Cheddar cheese
1 (8-ounce) package cream cheese (softened)
2 (7-ounce) jars chopped pimentos (drained)
1 (12-ounce) jar roasted red bell pepper (finely chopped)
¼ cup mayonnaise
2 tablespoons Worcestershire sauce
Dash of ground black pepper

1. Shred Cheddar cheeses with the size grater you prefer. (I use a midsize grater, so the cheese is the main thing I taste in the recipe.)
2. Simply mix the grated cheese mixture in with the remaining ingredients in a large bowl. Be careful to not mush the cheese into a lump; toss it as much as you stir it. Then, always, always, always, chill it overnight before you serve it.

HAND IT DOWN

My Big Mama made crocheted doll clothes for me at Christmas when I was a child. My Granny Hicks made George and me a beautiful quilt for our wedding day. There is nothing like homemade things. Yes, it takes lots of time—one stitch, then another. I made a hand-pieced quilt for Dallas and one for Hannah. It took me three years. I made William, Banks, and Cape "sheeties" with appliquéd figures made out of their outgrown clothes. Bay got a baby quilt that I made from antique white handkerchiefs, and Isabella got a quilt of all-white appliquéd animals. Why are handmade gifts so precious? Because they are made with love! If you have gifts like these, cherish them and pass them down. If not, think about who you could make a gift for to show your love.

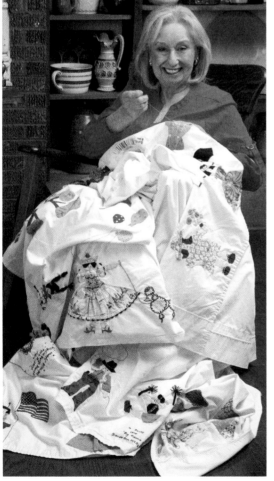

FRIED CHICKEN BITES

These are so easy to just pop in your mouth and enjoy. They're great for carrying on picnics, and of course, children love them, too! Don't forget to bring your favorite dipping sauce!

3   boneless skinless chicken breasts
½   teaspoon garlic salt
½   teaspoon ground black pepper
½   cup whole buttermilk
1½ cups White Lily all-purpose flour
Canola or vegetable oil
Ranch dressing

1. Trim fat and gristle from chicken breasts. Cut chicken into 1-inch cubes and put in a large bowl. Season with garlic salt and pepper. Add buttermilk and toss to coat chicken pieces. Refrigerate for several hours, if time permits. Remove from refrigerator and let stand at room temperature for about 20 minutes before you are ready to cook.

2. Remove chicken from buttermilk mixture, letting the excess drip off, and discard buttermilk mixture. Place flour in a large bowl.

3. Pour oil in a cast-iron skillet to fill about ¼ inch and heat over medium-high heat.

When oil is hot, place one handful chicken pieces into flour and toss to coat. Be sure to shake off excess flour; place a few chicken pieces at a time in oil. Repeat until skillet is three-fourths full. Do not overcrowd. Cook until chicken pieces are looking golden on one side, about 3 minutes. Using a fork, turn chicken pieces to the other side. Cook until golden brown, about 4 minutes. Remove with a slotted utensil and let drain on paper towels. Repeat steps until all chicken pieces are cooked. We like to serve ours with ranch dressing.

FOR SO IS THE WILL OF GOD, THAT WITH WELL DOING YE MAY PUT TO SILENCE THE IGNORANCE OF FOOLISH MEN.
—1 PETER 2:15, KJV

George as the grillmaster—that was his specialty

SHRIMP & FETA PASTA

When you put shrimp and pasta together, you have created a dish that will be a hit at any function. You can't go wrong. Make it the day before, and you'll be at ease the day of the picnic.

6 cups water
1 pound medium bite-size fresh shrimp
1 (12-ounce) box bow tie pasta
3 to 4 large carrots
½ cup finely chopped red bell pepper
½ cup mayonnaise
½ teaspoon garlic salt
½ teaspoon ground black pepper
½ lemon (juiced)
1 (4-ounce) container crumbled feta cheese

1. Bring 6 cups water to a hard boil. Drop in shrimp and cook for 3 minutes. Remove from heat and immediately drain. Peel shrimp.
2. Cook pasta according to package directions and drain well.
3. Peel and slice carrots. In a large pot, bring carrots and water to cover to a boil just until tender, about 7 to 8 minutes. Do not overcook. Drain well.
4. In a large bowl, combine shrimp, pasta, carrots, bell pepper, mayonnaise, garlic salt, black pepper, and lemon juice. Stir together. Add feta cheese and toss. Chill for several hours.

Walt and Banks bonding

William, Cape, Isabella, Bay, George, Dallas, and Banks

MASON JAR TRIFLE

———◆———

What a beautiful, handy dessert for a picnic. Just grab a jar and a spoon . . . enjoy! It's a true make-ahead dessert.

1   angel food cake (made from a box mix or store-bought)
3   cups cold whole milk
1   (5.1-ounce) box instant vanilla pudding mix
1   (8-ounce) container whipped topping
1   mango (peeled and diced)
2   kiwi (peeled and diced)
1½   cups thinly sliced fresh strawberries

1. Pinch up one-third cake and place pieces in the bottom of 5 or 6 Mason jars.
2. In a bowl, whisk together milk and pudding mix. Quickly add three-fourths of whipped topping. Pour a small amount of pudding mixture into each jar to lightly cover the top of the cake pieces. Add a few pieces of mango, kiwi, and strawberries to each jar. Repeat layers two more times.
3. Seal jars with lids and refrigerate until ready to serve.

KITCHEN WISDOM

You are going to have some pudding mixture left. If you only do two layers, you will be able to make six servings. If you do three layers, it will make five servings.

ROSEMARY & GARLIC BREAD

I grow rosemary all around my yard to have it on hand for cooking. Rosemary and garlic go so well together and give great flavor to breads and potato dishes.

1   (16-ounce) loaf crusty bread (sourdough or three-cheese from deli)
5   small sprigs fresh rosemary
1   stick salted butter (softened)
1   teaspoon garlic salt

1. Preheat oven to 350°.
2. Using a serrated knife, slice bread into about ¼-inch-thick slices. Do not go all the way through the loaf; cut down until only the bottom crust is holding the loaf together. Place on a large sheet of aluminum foil, large enough to loosely wrap the entire loaf.

3. Using kitchen shears, snip rosemary leaves from stems and chop into small pieces.
4. In a small bowl, mix butter, garlic salt, and rosemary together to make a paste.
5. Take a butter knife and spread mixture between each bread slice. If any of the mixture is left, spread on top of the loaf. Loosely wrap the foil over the top and ends of loaf.
6. Bake for 30 minutes.

FOR ALL FLESH IS AS GRASS, AND ALL THE GLORY OF MAN AS THE FLOWER OF GRASS. THE GRASS WITHERETH, AND THE FLOWER THEREOF FALLETH AWAY:
BUT THE WORD OF THE LORD ENDURETH FOR EVER. AND THIS IS THE WORD WHICH BY THE GOSPEL IS PREACHED UNTO YOU.
—1 PETER 1:24–25, KJV

KITCHEN WISDOM

When the bread is done, leave it wrapped in foil and put it in your picnic basket to keep it warm. Wait to pull it apart for everyone at the picnic.

DIRT SMELLS GOOD

All my life, I've loved the smell and feel of dirt, the wind blowing through the tall trees, the shrubs blooming and gracing the land, bulbs that pop up their heads to color the earth with their beauty, the wildflowers that just show up in the most unusual places, and fruit just hanging on the trees, ready for me to pick. Nature and plants have brought me joy and comfort during times I've been down and out. Their ever-changing form lets me know that life itself is ever-changing. Nothing stays the same.

Auburn University has a master gardener educational program. Hannah and I jumped aboard when she was pregnant with Bay, so I know it was about 20 years ago. They provided excellent teachers who taught our class about fertilizer, rooting, insects and pests, soil pH balance, vegetable gardening, rose pruning, and when to cut back blooming shrubs. These aren't all the subjects—there were many more!

At the end of each week, we had a test on the subject we had covered that week. Hannah and I passed! Hallelujah!

Even now, after 20 years, some of our happiest times are when Hannah and I are swapping plants, planting seeds, and rooting plants from other friends' gardens. My son, Dallas, also loves planting. He and Walt plant for the deer every year along with veggies for our family. Dallas has planted hundreds of trees, too.

God must love gardening, too. He put Adam and Eve right in the middle of a beautiful garden.

AND GOD SAID, BEHOLD, I HAVE GIVEN YOU EVERY HERB BEARING SEED, WHICH IS UPON THE FACE OF ALL THE EARTH, AND EVERY TREE, IN WHICH IS THE FRUIT OF A TREE YIELDING SEED, TO YOU IT SHALL BE FOR MEAT.
—GENESIS 1:29, KJV

AND THE LORD GOD TOOK THE MAN AND PUT HIM INTO THE GARDEN OF EDEN TO WORK IT AND KEEP IT.
—GENESIS 2:15, ESV

When I read the Bible, I find that there are many scriptures where the Lord talks about plants, water, rain, and fruits. I know that God has put in my being a love and desire to be outside among His creation! I taught science for many years—this was my very favorite subject because it was all about God's perfect creation—from orbits, solar systems, plant reproduction, water cycles, human bodies, and the earth itself! I never tire of spending time outside. It always fills my soul with a special joy and peace.

What a magnificent blessing we all have been given. Get outside and plant something! You will be amazed at how you will feel! Enjoy!

5-CUP FRUIT SALAD

What I like about this salad is that you can put the things your family likes in it. You can be as creative as you like.

1   (16-ounce) jar maraschino cherries
1   (15-ounce) can mandarin oranges
1   (20-ounce) can pineapple tidbits
1½   cups miniature marshmallows
1   cup chopped pecans
1   cup grated coconut
1   cup sour cream

1. Drain cherries, oranges, and pineapple and reserve all juices for 5-Cup Fruit Punch (recipe on page 227).
2. In a large bowl, mix cherries, oranges, pineapple, marshmallows, pecans, coconut, and sour cream, tossing until coated. Refrigerate until ready to serve.

5-CUP FRUIT PUNCH

Never drain your canned fruit juices down the sink. Save it all in a pitcher—add a little pink lemonade powder and, voilà, you have a refreshing punch.

Fruit juices reserved from 5-Cup Fruit Salad (recipe on page 226)
3 tablespoons pink lemonade drink mix
1 cup sugar
4 cups water

1. Mix all ingredients together. Fill your glass with ice and enjoy the refreshing taste!

George having a picnic of hot dogs and milk with Bay and Cape

THEREFORE TO HIM THAT
KNOWETH TO DO GOOD, AND
DOETH IT NOT, TO HIM IT IS SIN.
—JAMES 4:17, KJV

BROCCOLI SALAD

If you have never tried this salad, you have missed out. These ingredients mixed together are wonderful. Don't try to change this recipe—it's perfect the way it is!

1	large bunch broccoli, chopped (about 4 cups)
½	cup chopped red onion
½	cup dark raisins
½	cup chopped pecans
6	slices bacon (cooked and chopped)

Dressing:

1	cup mayonnaise
3	tablespoons white vinegar
⅓	cup sugar

1. In a large bowl, mix broccoli, onion, raisins, pecans, and bacon together.
2. In a small bowl, mix all dressing ingredients. Pour the dressing over the broccoli mixture right before serving and toss to completely coat.

Apron Strings

Remember, we get to choose how we're going to act and what our attitudes are going to be. Humans are good at blaming others, making excuses, and having negative reactions. But we don't have to be like everybody else. We can decide to be positive and take responsibility for our actions. It sets a good example for our children. Everybody makes mistakes, but the way you respond to mistakes is what's important in building character.

KITCHEN WISDOM

Sometimes, I like to toast my pecans to add extra flavor. In a cast-iron skillet over low heat, put just a little butter so the pecans don't stick, and pour in your pecans. Stir them around until they smell toasty—be sure not to let them burn!

chapter 10

SMALL-TOWN LIVING

SOMETHING SPECIAL

Small-town living is special! People are warm and welcoming everywhere you go. It's common to see people hugging, smiling, shaking hands, and praying together. Small-town living will lift your spirits. The cars cruise by slowly, no honking horns, and no bad looks. The stores are small and privately owned. Most of the time, it's the store owner who helps you find what you need.

Our town square bustles with pep rallies, picnics, craft shows, antique cars, Christmas parades, and teenagers just hanging out. It's wonderful to be a part of it all. Our churches have all kinds of activities and heartfelt worship services. They are continually hosting events for people of all ages. There are senior groups, Vacation Bible School, revivals, weddings, homecomings, graduation activities, fall festivals, concerts, and many churches even have a special night of eating for the entire town or whoever wants to come. The proceeds from these nights always go to a project or group in our area. There's Italian night, bayou feast, and fish fry, to name a few.

I imagine that folks who live in large cities think that there would be absolutely nothing to do in a small town. Well, folks, there are so many activities to do that I can't attend them all. But one thing is for sure—no matter what event we decide to go to in our small town, we will know most of the people there. If you live in a big city, you can create a community feeling through your church, community center, or other organizations—it just might take a little work, but it's worth it!

Change happens whether we like it or not. Time marches on. You can either get left behind or move forward. There is no middle ground. Just stop or go. I choose to go—change for the better. Be active, try new things, connect with my family and with my town. The old saying says absence makes the heart grow fonder. I say that is not true! When we communicate and spend time with family and friends, our bond grows stronger.

If you live, it's for sure that you're going to get old. But you don't have to feel old. Stay active in your town. Find like-minded people. Join a Bible study. Take classes and check out all the activities in your town to see which you are most comfortable with. Strangers are just people you haven't spoken to yet! Smile and speak!

The recipes in this chapter come from Andalusia, Alabama, townsfolk. These are some of our favorite recipes that we like to make when we get together for special occasions. I hope you'll love making them when you gather with your community.

SOURDOUGH BREAD

Jennifer Dansby

Jennifer has been using the same bread dough starter for 30 years. She's also been making bread and giving it away for 30 years . . . to visitors at First Baptist Church, to parents with new babies in the house, to folks who experience a death in the family, or just because she loves you! God has given her this ministry, and she is obedient to His call. This recipe makes two loaves and has been adapted to use commercial yeast you can buy at the grocery store, but if you've got starter, that's even better!

6½ cups bread flour
2 (0.25-ounce) packages active dry yeast
½ cup sugar
2 teaspoons salt
2 cups warm water (105° to 110°)
½ cup vegetable oil

1. In a large bowl, whisk together flour, yeast, sugar, and salt. Add 2 cups warm water and oil, whisking until combined. Cover with plastic wrap that has been sprayed with cooking spray. Let stand at least 8 hours.
2. Knead dough on a floured surface for 2 to 3 minutes. Divide dough in half and place each portion in a glass loaf pan that has been sprayed with cooking spray.

Loosely cover with plastic wrap that has been sprayed with cooking spray. Let rise in a warm place, free from drafts, for about 1 hour and 30 minutes or until smooth on top and springs back when pressed with a finger.
3. Preheat oven to 350°.
4. Uncover and bake until golden brown, about 45 minutes, covering with foil during last 5 minutes.

This gang of girls spent the week at the beach. We shopped, played table games, and ate lots of Sourdough Bread with tons of butter. Hope the clothes we bought will still fit after all the buttered bread!

A LETTER FROM
MRS. MARY HELEN THIGPEN
[OCTOBER 17, 2012]

Dear Brenda,

Thank you so very much for that sweet note. I love to decorate at old Jungle Nook—that old place has been part of my life since 1936. If I had the money I would have fun doing a whole lot of restoration and decoration. When I was growing up, I wanted to get away and see the world but now a glass of tea or a cup of coffee on the front porch with family and friends is where I like to be.

Ever since the Sunday when George told us you were gone because your mother had died, my heart has been in sympathy with you. I'm so sorry you had to lose her. It is sad and painful when we have to lose our mothers, no matter how old they are or we are.

Now you have your father to care for and he, like me, is one of the "old, old." (I heard if you are past 80, you are old, old.) We old ones hate to give up our independence, and we worry about being burdens on our children. But all we can do is pray about the sacrifices our children have to make and try to wake up every morning with a happy heart. God's plan is not always easy to follow, but we know it can lead us to Heaven!

And my advice to you is the same as it is to your daddy. Wake up every morning with a happy heart. Please repeat my advice to Julie after I'm gone. —MH

I felt a need to share this letter to me from Mrs. Mary Helen Thigpen, who was part of our small-town community. Getting old is not easy when you are a person who enjoys doing things for others. I've always liked to be right in the middle of all the action.

Mary Helen shows us all that we are valuable right up to the very end. She was full of wisdom and love for all who met her. I was encouraged by her wise words in this letter to me. It's telling me, don't give up! Get up each morning with a happy heart, and share that happy heart with those around you. We all should write kind and encouraging notes to others. This note was written to me 10 years ago. I've kept it in my Bible all this time.

Mary Helen went to be with the Lord in February 2022, and I mailed this note to her daughter, Julie. Why? Because this is what Mary Helen asked me to do. I'm reminding Julie, as her mother reminded me, to wake up every morning with a happy heart.

DESIRES

Have you ever had a desire to do a particular thing but never got around to it or never had the opportunity? I have. Ice-skating was one of those desires for me.

When I was a freckle-faced little girl and all through my teenage years, my mama took me, my brothers, and as many neighborhood kids as she could pack in the car to the local skating rink. We learned to skate backward, forward, and with a partner.

Now, in my old age, I long to skate again with the wind in my face—but no, if I fall, I might break a hip. It's funny how the desires we have still burn strong even when our bodies are older. In our heart, we feel young and still want to conquer the world, but these older bodies sing a different tune.

I'm thankful that our small town plans activities that all ages can enjoy. One of these activities is our July Jamz event. Every Thursday in July around 5 p.m., we start gathering at Springdale Estate. Mamas and daddies carry babies on their hips and in strollers. Young children run around arm in arm like a herd of caribou. And here come the teenagers, strutting around in their oh-so-cool outfits! Last, but not least, come the "old-agers."

We are not walking quite as fast as the others—kind of like the story of the slow-moving turtle against the fast-moving hare in the race to the finish line. We old ones get there one step at a time.

The lawn is adorned with quilts, fold-up chairs, and blankets. People from all over the county are talking, visiting, and laughing. We are all there for a summer night of free entertainment and fellowship. Local artists perform their magic as they sing and play their guitars, banjos, harmonicas, and drums—sometimes, folks get up off their quilts and begin to dance! Our feet just have to stomp when the music starts. I know for sure that the Lord put rhythm in our nature to love music.

To wind down the night, the city puts on a great fireworks display. We lie on the lawn and watch the night sky light up. Roller-skating will never happen for me again—ice-skating is out, too! But I will glory in the fact that I can enjoy watching the young ones. Joy is in my heart, not in the activity anyway!

July Jamz in Andalusia, Alabama

PUMPKIN SWIRL BREAD
Rosemary Gantt

Rosemary has a beautiful kitchen—she uses it to do lots of baking that others benefit from. She's an excellent cook who always makes something delicious to share with those around her. She even makes huge pots of soup and freezes it in zip-top bags just to give away.

1 (8-ounce) package cream cheese (softened)
1¾ cups sugar, divided
2 large eggs (lightly beaten), divided
1¾ cups White Lily all-purpose flour
1 teaspoon baking powder
½ teaspoon salt
1 teaspoon ground cinnamon
¼ teaspoon ground nutmeg
1 cup canned pumpkin
½ cup salted butter (melted)
⅓ cup water

1. Preheat oven to 350°. Lightly grease and flour a 9x5-inch loaf pan.

2. In a bowl, beat cream cheese, ¼ cup sugar, and 1 egg with a mixer at medium speed until blended. Set aside.

3. In a bowl, combine remaining 1½ cups sugar, flour, baking powder, salt, cinnamon, and nutmeg. Set aside.

4. In a separate bowl, combine pumpkin, butter, remaining 1 egg, and ⅓ cup water. Add flour mixture to pumpkin mixture, mixing just until moistened. Reserve 2 cups batter.

5. Pour remaining batter into prepared loaf pan. Pour cream cheese mixture over batter and top with reserved batter. Run a knife through batter to create a swirl.

6. Bake until a wooden pick inserted in the center comes out clean, 1 hour and 10 minutes. Let cool in the pan for 10 minutes and then remove to a wire rack to let cool completely.

KITCHEN WISDOM

This recipe can easily be doubled using one full can of pumpkin. You can make up several loaves to give away at Christmas or Thanksgiving.

CANDIED BACON WITH A KICK

Aubrey McKee

Aubrey is a singer, entertainer, and great party planner. But what I love about her is her kindness to others. She loves people. This is a delicious recipe that everybody loves. We always serve it at bridal and baby showers.

½   cup light brown sugar
½   cup chopped pecans
2   teaspoons kosher salt
1   teaspoon ground black pepper
⅛   teaspoon ground red pepper
2   tablespoons pure maple syrup
½   pound thick-cut bacon
     (about 8 slices)

1. Preheat oven to 400°. Line a rimmed baking sheet with aluminum foil and place a wire rack inside.

2. Combine brown sugar and pecans in a food processor and process until the mixture is finely ground. Add salt, black pepper, and red pepper and pulse to combine. Add maple syrup and pulse until mixture is moistened.

3. Cut each bacon slice in half and line up the pieces on the wire rack with some space between each. Spread pecan mixture on top of each piece of bacon.

4. Bake until topping is very browned but not burned, 25 to 30 minutes. (We're going for caramelized here. If it's undercooked, the bacon won't crisp as it cools.) While bacon is still hot, transfer the pieces to a paper towel and let cool.

Brenda and Aubrey

BUT BE YE DOERS OF THE WORD, AND NOT HEARERS ONLY,

DECEIVING YOUR OWN SELVES.

—JAMES 1:22, KJV

PEANUT BUTTER BALLS
Era Andrews

Era is one of Bethany Baptist Church's best cooks. She's been cooking for about 80 years. Open houses at Christmastime and taking platters of goodies to folks give her so much pleasure.

2   sticks salted butter (melted)
1½ cups creamy peanut butter
1½ cups graham cracker crumbs
1   box powdered sugar
1   teaspoon vanilla extract
1   (12-ounce) package milk chocolate chips
3   (1.55-ounce) milk chocolate candy bars
½   block food-grade paraffin wax

1. In a bowl, mix melted butter and peanut butter together. In another bowl, mix together cracker crumbs, sugar, and vanilla. Add peanut butter mixture and stir until combined. Using a 2-teaspoon scoop, scoop mixture and roll into balls. Chill.

2. Using a double boiler, melt the chocolate chips, candy bars, and paraffin. Using a fork, dip the balls in the melted chocolate mixture. Place on parchment paper or wax paper. Let cool before serving.

COCONUT-ALMOND CANDY
Era Andrews

You will find candy on Era's Christmas platter, if you are one of the lucky ones. She cooks the old-time way—sight, taste, feeling, and smell. It gives her the perfect dish every time. We could all learn a thing or two from her.

2   sticks salted butter
1   (14-ounce) can sweetened condensed milk
2   (14-ounce) bags sweetened flaked coconut
1   can whole unsalted almonds (about 86)
2   (12-ounce) packages milk chocolate chips
1   block food-grade paraffin wax

1. In a small pot, heat butter and condensed milk over low heat until the butter is melted. Add coconut, stirring to combine. Let cool completely. (This is important, as you cannot work with it unless it is cold. I usually leave mine overnight.)

2. Using a 2-teaspoon scoop, scoop coconut mixture and shape into a ball around individual almonds.

3. Using a double boiler, melt the chocolate chips and paraffin. Using a fork, dip the balls in the melted chocolate mixture. Place on parchment paper or wax paper. Let cool before serving.

DEEP-DISH PIZZA

Nikki Bodie

Nikki and I met when she was teaching my Hannah in kindergarten. Mrs. Bodie gave Hannah great memories of her first school experience. That's when she gave me this easy recipe. I've been making it for about 40 years. It's a winner.

1   (16.3-ounce) can refrigerated flaky-layers biscuits (8 count)
2   (14-ounce) jars pizza sauce
1   pound ground sausage (cooked and drained)
1   onion (sliced very thin)
1   (8-ounce) can sliced mushrooms (drained)
1   small bell pepper (sliced very thin)
3   cups grated mozzarella cheese

1. Preheat oven to 400°. Grease an 11x9-inch casserole dish.
2. Separate biscuit layers and arrange in bottom and up sides of prepared dish, pressing with fingers to close the gaps for a solid crust.
3. Spread 1 jar pizza sauce over crust. Layer with half of sausage, onion, mushrooms, bell pepper, and cheese. Top with remaining sausage, onion, mushrooms, and bell pepper. Top with remaining jar pizza sauce and remaining cheese. Cover with a piece of foil simply laying on top of the dish, not tucked in tight.
4. Bake for 40 minutes. Remove foil and bake until crust is browned, 10 more minutes.

THEREFORE I SAY UNTO YOU, TAKE NO THOUGHT FOR YOUR LIFE, WHAT YE SHALL EAT, OR WHAT YE SHALL DRINK; NOR YET FOR YOUR BODY, WHAT YE SHALL PUT ON. IS NOT THE LIFE MORE THAN MEAT, AND THE BODY THAN RAIMENT?
—MATTHEW 6:25, KJV

KITCHEN WISDOM

Serve with a simple salad made with tomatoes, cucumber, and romaine lettuce to get more veggies into your meal.

ORANGE CAKE
Jewel Curry

———◆———

Mrs. Jewel has baked hundreds of these cakes over the years and has had the joy of teaching her granddaughters to make it, as well. She always made her famous Orange Cake when there was a death in her family or in her church family. What a blessing she has been to so many.

1 (15.25-ounce) box orange cake mix
1 (3-ounce) box coconut cream pudding mix
1 cup vegetable oil
4 large eggs
1 (12-ounce) can lemon-lime soda

Icing:
1 (20-ounce) can crushed pineapple
1½ cups sugar
1 stick salted butter
3 tablespoons cornstarch
1½ cups chopped toasted pecans

1. Preheat oven to 350°. Grease and flour 5 (8-inch) cake pans. (If you don't have 5 pans, you can bake a few at a time and allow the remaining dough to rest.)
2. Beat all ingredients with a mixer at medium speed until well blended.
3. Bake about 12 minutes. Let cool before icing.

1. Combine pineapple, sugar, butter, and cornstarch in a heavy boiler; bring to boil over medium heat, stirring often. Cook until bubbling and thickened. Let cool completely.
2. When icing is cool, spread between each cake layer and on top of cake, sprinkling each layer with pecans.

Mrs. Maryanne Murphy's annual Easter egg hunt for her ballet students

Brenda and friends at First Baptist in Andalusia, Alabama

CHOCOLATE SHEET CAKE

Bessie Hare Riley

—◆—

Bessie carried this cake to church gatherings and always made it when her family was going to be at her house—her grandchildren loved it! The ingredients are items she would have on hand, so she could make it in a moment's notice.

2 cups White Lily self-rising flour
2 cups sugar
4 tablespoons cocoa powder
2 sticks salted butter
1 cup water
2 large eggs (slightly beaten)
¼ cup whole buttermilk
1 teaspoon vanilla extract

Icing:
1 stick salted butter
4 tablespoons cocoa powder
6 or 8 tablespoons whole milk
1 box powdered sugar
1 cup chopped pecans
1 teaspoon vanilla extract

1. Preheat oven to 350°. Grease an 11x9-inch baking dish.
2. In a large bowl, sift together flour, sugar, and cocoa.
3. In a small pan, bring butter and 1 cup water to a boil over medium heat. Pour butter mixture over flour mixture. Stir in eggs, buttermilk, and vanilla. Pour into prepared dish.
4. Bake until a wooden pick comes out clean, 35 to 40 minutes.

1. Make icing while cake is still warm. In a medium pot, bring butter, cocoa, and milk to a boil over medium heat. Stir in powdered sugar, pecans, and vanilla. Pour icing over warm cake.

Bessie Hare Riley with her granddaughter, Shonna, and great-granddaughter, Rachel

THE LORD IS MY STRENGTH
AND SONG, AND IS BECOME
MY SALVATION.
—PSALM 118:14, KJV

PEANUT BUTTER CORNFLAKES CANDY

Laquetta Grimes

Talk about a worker! Laquetta can get a meal together in no time! She is a great cook—I guess she has to be with eight grandchildren. She and her husband, Jeff, worked with George and me to cook one Wednesday night meal a month at Bethany Baptist Church for almost 10 years. She and I shared cooking secrets and kept our husbands peeling potatoes!

1   cup sugar
1   cup corn syrup
1   (12-ounce) container creamy peanut butter
6   cups cornflakes cereal

1. In large pan, bring sugar and corn syrup to a boil over medium heat. Continue boiling a few minutes until mixture looks clear. Remove from heat and add peanut butter. Stir until well blended. Then add cornflakes, stirring until well combined.

2. Scoop cornflakes mixture and use your hands to form into about 1-inch balls. Place on parchment or wax paper and let stand until set. Store in an airtight container.

BAKED SALMON
Maria Thigpen

I've eaten many meals at Bill and Maria's home. She always serves a delicious meal. We met years ago when they'd shop with us at our store, Sweetgum Bottom Antiques. They would buy some treasures, then George and I would sit on the porch and talk with them until closing time.

2   tablespoons olive oil
1   teaspoon garlic powder or minced fresh garlic
¼   teaspoon salt
¼   teaspoon ground black pepper
½   teaspoon chopped dill (dried or fresh)
4   (6-ounce) fresh salmon fillets

1. Preheat oven to 375°. Grease a baking sheet with olive oil.
2. In a small bowl, mix together garlic powder, salt, pepper, and dill. Rub each salmon fillet with garlic mixture. Place salmon, skin side down, on a prepared pan.
3. Bake for about 15 minutes.

IRON SKILLET POUND CAKE
Jo Ellen Sellers

Jo Ellen is the most real person you will ever meet. Her soft-spoken words and that unforgettable laugh will put even the most uptight person at ease! I love this Iron Skillet Pound Cake—it's great for any meal, even breakfast.

2 sticks unsalted butter, melted
1½ cups sugar
3 large eggs, room temperature
1¼ cups White Lily all-purpose flour
1 teaspoon salt
1 teaspoon vanilla extract
Whipped cream
Fresh fruit

1. Preheat oven to 300°. Spray a 10-inch cast-iron skillet with cooking spray.

2. Beat melted butter and sugar with a mixer at medium speed. Add eggs, one at a time, beating at medium speed just until combined. Add flour and salt; beat at medium speed for 3 minutes. Add vanilla and mix well. Pour batter into prepared skillet.

3. Bake for about 1 hour. (I do not cook mine for an hour; begin checking cake after 40 minutes, as all ovens bake differently.) Serve out of the skillet and top with whipped cream and fruit. Delicious!

Apron Strings

My advice to others is to watch and be ready for God to open a door for you—then walk through it. The Lord, also, will close doors. Be ready for that, too. Don't worry when He closes a door! He will open another.

KITCHEN WISDOM

I like to add fresh blueberries, strawberries, pecans, peaches, or blackberries to the batter or on top.

STARTING OVER

Jackie, Brenda, and Neil at July Jamz

After George passed away in September 2018, I found myself trying to make heads or tails of my life. The last two years of George's life were stressful for us both, to say the least. Now, I had to get hold of myself and start over. After 50 wonderful years of marriage to my sweetheart and soul mate, I felt this wouldn't come easy, but I had so much to live for. My Lord would guide; I must start over!

Covington County has so many exciting things to do and opportunities to make new memories. The first thing I did was to start back to church. I couldn't leave George alone when he was sick, so the only time I had gotten to go to church was when our children kept him. Worship was hard at first—I cried almost the whole service. Bible study came next. We ladies met together for refreshments, hugs, and study. What more could I ask for?

A friend told me about the Silver Sneakers program, and I signed up. This allowed me to go to the gym and work out—you should have seen me on the machinery, especially the bench press! I imagine that all the young folks in the gym were laughing behind my back. Good thing I'm old enough now that it doesn't bother me at all!

Then came some line dancing, day adventure trips, and getaways with friends. Bethany Gold senior functions—Wednesday night supper and prayer meetings at church—God was opening doors everywhere I looked. George wanted me to live, to care for myself and the family. So, by being active in our small-town community, I learned to walk forward and not look back.

At night when all is quiet and dark, I think of my George and how I miss him so. I'm thankful for the Lord's constant presence in my life. His love will never end. My children and grandchildren are my strongest supporters, my encouragers, and my loves. I'm thankful, too, for my small town full of loving people who truly care.

If you're starting over, look for opportunities and activities you can sign up for. Which friends and family members can you invite to sit around the table with you? The Lord always provides a way forward. Be ready and willing.

EDITOR'S NOTE When you visit Mrs. Brenda in Andalusia, Alabama, you can't help but notice the number of tables in her home. She has a large dining room table that her husband, George, built from trees on their land, a kitchen table that's been passed down for generations, a table in her den that seats six (this is where the book team eats when we're in town since the other tables are piled high with food and equipment!), a table on the front porch, a table on the back patio, and a picnic table in the backyard. And, this isn't even counting all of her sitting areas where people can gather or the four other tables across the street at The Cottle House Bed & Breakfast! It doesn't take long to realize that gathering around a table over good food and conversation is important to Mrs. Brenda. When we arrive to work on her books, she always greets us with food and asks us to sit down for a minute and talk. We chat about our families, our work, and our communities. For Mrs. Brenda, a table—whether a beautifully adorned dining room table, a simple outdoor picnic table, or the Communion table—is about connection. That's what she wants for her readers, and that's why she advises you to linger. Stay a little longer—catch up with an old friend, laugh with your family at stories you've heard a million times, or reminisce with loved ones about holidays and celebrations of the past. The dishes can wait. —Anna Hartzog

RECIPE INDEX

RESOURCES

Follow Brenda Gantt on Facebook at *facebook.com/cookingwithbrendagantt.*

To find writings by Walt Merrell, follow Shepherding Outdoors on Facebook at *facebook.com/shepherdingoutdoors.*

For more information about The Cottle House, visit *hickoryridgelodge.com.*

To find White Lily products, visit *whitelily.com.*

For more information on Andalusia, Alabama, visit *cityofandalusia.com.*

All personal photography was provided by Brenda Gantt.

EDITORIAL

**Chairman of the Board/
Chief Executive Officer**
Phyllis Hoffman DePiano

President/Chief Creative Officer
Brian Hart Hoffman

VP/Culinary & Custom Content
Brooke Michael Bell

Group Creative Director
Deanna Rippy Gardner

Senior Project Editor Anna Hartzog

Project Editors Barbara McCarthy
and Lauren Gentry Walker

Copy Editor Adrienne Davis

Test Kitchen Director Laura Crandall

Food Stylists Vanessa Rocchio and
Kathleen Kanen

Senior Stylist Sidney Bragiel

Stylist Lucy Finney

Creative Director/Photography
Mac Jamieson

Photographer Jim Bathie

COVER

Photography by Jim Bathie
Styling by Sidney Bragiel and
Vanessa Rocchio

PRODUCTION & MARKETING

EVP/Operations and Manufacturing
Greg Baugh

VP/Digital Media Jon Adamson

Marketing Director Kristy Harrison

A SPECIAL THANK YOU

Well, y'all, we did it again! I am so proud of this cookbook and all the work that went into it. It would not have been possible without the support of my family. I'm thankful for my children and grandchildren who offered their opinions, direction, and love as we worked to create a book that reflects our lives and our mission. Hannah devoted many hours to helping me proofread, and I am so appreciative of her help. I am grateful to my community here in Andalusia, Alabama, who've given support—especially Shonna Reeves, Gloria Day, Mary Lynn Stone, Maria Thigpen, JoEllen Sellers, Julie Wells, my friends who shared recipes for the "Small-Town Living" chapter, and my line dancing class. Thank you to my sweet friends of more than 50 years from Livingston State College, Pam Burgess, Andrea Holms, and Carole Henry, who traveled from all over the state to be in Andalusia with me for a Christmas photo shoot—who would have thought 50 years ago, this is where we'd be now?

Thank you to my friends at Hoffman Media: Sidney, who styles everything just right (one centimeter at a time) and keeps my hair in place; Vanessa, who helps cook all my recipes, makes the food look delicious, and keeps everyone laughing in the kitchen; Jim, who takes the pictures and is sure to get my good side; Anna, who edits my stories and keeps the project (and me!) on track; Deanna, who takes all the many pieces of our project and crafts them into a book; and everyone else on the Hoffman Media team who works behind the scenes to make something so special to me and so beautiful for the readers.

—Brenda

Dear Lord,

I'm in the winter of my life looking back over all the years we have been together. I've seen and felt you moving and taking loving care of me through the deep valleys. You've given joy and blessings all along the way.

I've had regrets, and my sins are ever before me. But, oh what comfort it is to be forgiven of each and every downfall. As I continue through this time of old age, Lord, guide me and help me to cherish each moment that's laid out before me.

George has gone to be with you. The children are grown with children of their own. They are working hard and managing their families. It's such a comfort to know that you are always faithful in your love for us all. We will never be alone —Lord, you are always there. You lift us up and give us strength. You restore our hearts and souls. So, in the winter days that are cold and gray, I praise you, Lord, for being my sunshine, my glory, and my light in the darkness of this world.

Lord, my prayer is that this simple cookbook will somehow touch the lives of the ones who hold it in their hands. I pray that they will feel the peace and love that you offer. The old rugged cross could not hold you. The grave could not hold you. Praise be to you, God, you made a way for us to be with you for eternity.

I'm in awe of your love.

Your child,
Brenda